T0114703

READING AND UNDERSTANDING
RESEARCH ARTICLES

A Quick Guide for Yoga
Teachers and Practitioners

ETHAN EK SEE, PhD

BALBOA.PRESS
A DIVISION OF HAY HOUSE

Balboa Press books may be ordered through booksellers or by contacting:

Balboa Press
A Division of Hay House
1663 Liberty Drive
Bloomington, IN 47403
www.balboapress.com
844-682-1282

Because of the dynamic nature of the Internet, any web addresses or links contained in this book may have changed since publication and may no longer be valid. The views expressed in this work are solely those of the author and do not necessarily reflect the views of the publisher, and the publisher hereby disclaims any responsibility for them.

The author of this book does not dispense medical advice or prescribe the use of any technique as a form of treatment for physical, emotional, or medical problems without the advice of a physician, either directly or indirectly. The intent of the author is only to offer information of a general nature to help you in your quest for emotional and spiritual well-being. In the event you use any of the information in this book for yourself, which is your constitutional right, the author and the publisher assume no responsibility for your actions.

Any people depicted in stock imagery provided by Getty Images are models, and such images are being used for illustrative purposes only. Certain stock imagery © Getty Images.

Print information available on the last page.

ISBN: 979-8-7652-4621-4 (sc)
ISBN: 979-8-7652-4622-1 (e)

Balboa Press rev. date: 10/18/2023

DEDICATION

This book is dedicated to all my academic professors and yoga teachers who have taught me and all my students who have studied with me. All of you have enabled me to become a better teacher as well as combine my love of research literacy, yoga, and complementary modalities in my life. Thank you.

PREFACE

Why do we read research articles on yoga?

Yoga has become a global phenomenon and force for well-being and transformation. There are now numerous yoga centers worldwide providing yoga classes and yoga teacher training. As yoga becomes more and more popular and gains mainstream acceptance in various institutions such as schools and workplaces, it is imperative for us to understand the impact in more tangible terms. One important way to understand this impact is through research articles found in academic journals.

Most benefits about yoga most yoga practitioners probably know might be from what they have read in magazine articles, health websites or from conversations with their friend. Of course, there is nothing wrong with gleaning the main takeaway from a research article. It is, however, beneficial for you, as a yoga teacher and practitioner, to know how the research came about, so that you have a more holistic understanding of research. More research articles have now become open access, meaning that it is made available to the public, free of charge. Today, you don't have to work for or study at a journal-subscribing institution in order to gain access to some journal articles. You now have the opportunity to read the research on your own, first-hand. This book is written for you so that you can navigate your way through a research article effectively.

As a yoga teacher or practitioner, it is highly useful to know whether what you are teaching and/or practising is informed by some research. Knowing the research process that yields a particular finding helps you to explain the benefits and implications to a client more convincingly. Most people are confounded by a research article in terms of its sheer amount of information and the language. This book helps you to understand a research article in an organized manner and appreciate how the language used in these articles facilitates the communication of research.

Moreover, it is highly beneficial for you to enrich yourself so that you can become a more discerning consumer of research. In the present world, many people are content producers, but they may not have the credibility nor expertise to produce content on a particular topic or interpret a finding. Imagine if someone puts forward on social media, a controversial claim about yoga based on a research study they have read. You can always refer to the relevant research article to check if they have communicated the research accurately. Knowing the full context of a research study on various topics makes you a knowledgeable teacher or practitioner who can engage in productive discussions with others.

Fourth, enriching yourself means you are part of a discourse community sharing the same language and knowledge core. This implies that you can discuss research and practice with other practitioners more meaningfully. At some point, you may be involved in designing and carrying out research on yoga or complementary modalities. Therefore, this forms an important part of your knowledge and skills set.

How to read this book

This book is written in 8 short chapters. It is most beneficial to read the book in a sequential manner. Chapter 1 provides a relevant backdrop to the research article by outlining the research process. This helps you to understand concisely how researchers think about and work through a research study. In addition, it surveys the various genres that are found in the commercial and research arena. Researchers refer to some of these sources during the course of their research. Chapters 2, 3 and 4 cover the various rhetorical elements found in the Introduction, Methodology and Results & Discussion sections of a Research Article. Chapter 5 covers the Conclusion, Abstract and other rhetorical elements of a research article. Chapter 6 explains how citations and references work in a research article. Chapter 7 describes the language of research writing, and you are unlikely to view research writing or any form of writing the same way again. Chapter 8 concludes and summarizes the main points that are covered. This chapter is subsequently followed by a review quiz.

You may, of course, choose to read the book in any order. For example, you may wish to start right away with learning to read a research article. Chapter 2 will be a good place to start. However, it would be advantageous to read Chapter 1 at some point before the other chapters so that you have a clear understanding of the culture and process of research.

Throughout this book, the examples are taken from Yoga research articles. I have provided a bibliography of these works at the end of the book. You should be able to download the research articles referred to in this book by searching for the DOI numbers online. In fact, it will supplement your learning greatly if you download a research article to view its overall structure. Throughout the writing in this book, I have also adhered to the APA (American Psychological Association) citation style as I find it conducive to the teaching and learning of the content. The APA system is an author-year system of citation. Most yoga research articles tend to use a numerical system of citation.

For continuing education on a related course on understanding research articles for yoga teachers, please reach out via the following means:

Website email: info@nlpyogawell.com
Website: https://nlpyogawell.com
Instructor's email: drethansee@gmail.com

As you read this book, I wish you the best in enjoying the learning journey.

TABLE OF CONTENTS

Chapter 1: Understanding the Research
            Process and Genres.....................................1

Chapter 2: Research Articles - Introduction 15

Chapter 3: Research Articles – Methodology 29

Chapter 4: Research Articles – Results & Discussion.........47

Chapter 5: Research Articles – Conclusion,
            Abstract and Other Rhetorical Elements 69

Chapter 6: Research Articles –
            Citations and References.......................................81

Chapter 7: The Language of Research Articles....................89

Chapter 8: Consolidation... 103

Review Quiz 107

Answers to Review Quiz 117

Continuing Education...119

Bibliography... 121

About the Author 123

CHAPTER 1

UNDERSTANDING THE RESEARCH PROCESS AND GENRES

Research Process

What is research?

When the word 'research' comes up in conversation, it is usually in the context of what research has found. Indeed, whether we are aware of it or not, our lives are strongly impacted in some way by the insights that research offers. The medication that you are taking is the result of scientific research and breakthroughs. The products that are being rolled out to customers are also informed by consumer research. The education programs and curricula in schools have been informed by research.

So, what is research? According to the online Merriam-Webster Dictionary, research is defined as "investigation or experimentation aimed at the discovery and interpretation of facts, revision of accepted theories or laws in the light of new facts, or practical application of such new or revised theories or laws" (Merriam-Webster, 2023). By far, this is one of the most comprehensive definitions I have come across.

It aligns with major parts of the research procedures used by researchers, namely examining or testing to derive new insights, comparing with existing knowledge about the subject matter or topic, and recommending application of insights. What needs to be further emphasized too that in order to generate new knowledge, researchers also adhere to well-planned data collection procedures and rigorous data analysis and interpretation to answer the research question.

Put simply, the research process can be described in the following way. You may have a question about a particular topic, issue or phenomenon, for example, about yoga. You then endeavor to answer the question through collecting data and analyzing them using appropriate methods. Thereafter, you interpret and evaluate the findings. Finally, you arrive at a conclusion about the topic.

In this regard, the process can be sequentially represented as follows:

- Research question formulation
- Literature Review
- Methodology: Data Collection
- Analysis and Interpretation
- Conclusion

Here is an example of a possible research process. In the first place, how does a researcher decide on a research topic? Researchers usually work in a particular field or a subject matter. They may be sport scientists who are interested in the impact of yoga. Or they may be medical doctors who are interested in finding out which breathing method in yoga can be a beneficial complementary modality to help their patients manage their anxiety problems. Another possibility is that they could be humanities and social science scholars trying to analyse how yoga students feel about yoga in their daily routines. Very often, people who conduct research on yoga are yoga practitioners or yoga teachers themselves. Based on their own research interests and yoga practices, they may formulate certain research questions about certain aspects of yoga.

For example, a group of researchers may be interested to find out about the high school students' perceptions of yoga programs that are conducted in public schools to help them cope with stress. First, researchers will scour past literature, especially research journals, to find out what has been done in this area of study. This step is very important because someone else might have already conducted this research, and this may not be considered a new study if all the variables are the same. Researchers place a huge emphasis on originality so that they can create new knowledge and push the boundaries of research.

After deciding on the research topic and objective, the researchers decide on the exact research questions to answer.

> RQ1: What aspects of the yoga program are useful for the students in managing stress in school?

> RQ2: Which aspects of the yoga program are not useful for the students in managing stress in school?

> RQ3: What do students think about the quality of the teaching in the yoga program?

In order to answer this research question, the researchers need to collect the relevant data. The research objective/

question guides their choice of research method. They have a few options.

Do they wish to conduct a survey in which the researchers fill out a questionnaire? This will yield a lot of quantitative data as the participants will usually indicate their response to series of questions on a scale. Are they more concerned in treating this research as an exploratory or pilot study? Their main aim here then is to gather as much qualitative data as possible to understand the depth of experience of the yoga class. Therefore, the researchers may choose to conduct focus group interviews or in-depth interviews with a sample of participants.

Yet, some researchers may choose to use mixed methods, meaning using a combination of the above methods so that they get both quantitative and qualitative data. Of course, these decisions also hinge on their available resources, which is why a lot of large-scale research is sponsored by research grants. Another important consideration is whether the researchers have access to the research venue and participants. Some organisations are protective of their programs and students, so there is no way to conduct the research then. The researchers have to find other suitable participants or research sites, if possible.

Of course, surveys are not the only way to gather information. If the researchers' aim is to investigate the efficacy of yoga nidra on the sleeping patterns of insomniac patients, then the more appropriate method of gathering the data is to objectively measure the sleeping hours and brain activity using appropriate medical equipment. For this research objective, the researchers will not be able to use surveys because these are meant to measure perceptions and attitudes of participants. Of course, researchers can sometimes request participants to take notes on their habits. In research such as those investigating habits (e.g., eating and drinking), researchers may ask participants to make an entry in their diaries. In these cases, the participants would be briefed about the method of recording the habits because research is required to have a large degree of systematicity.

Some research questions lend themselves to an investigation via experiments. Experiments do not necessarily mean the mixing of chemicals in a laboratory. If the research objective is to examine the impact of a hatha yoga session on concentration, researchers may then assign participants in two different groups. Group 1 participants will complete the concentration task without yoga whereas Group 2 will undergo the yoga session before completing a similar task. This type of research design is known as an experiment. Group 1 is known as a control group whereas Group 2 is known as an experimental group. This is a rather simple explanation of this type of design. Other factors need to be kept consistent or controlled in order for this study to be valid. In cases like these, researchers may come up with a hypothesis which is an educated guess about the outcome. They may state that the yoga has a significant impact on participants' concentration.

In addition, researchers also decide on the method they use in order to analyze the data. This stage is also known as "Analysis". They may use statistical calculations, tabulations, and analysis such as mean, T-tests, ANOVA, MANOVA, etc. in a quantitative study. The calculations are usually done on well-known software such as Excel and SPSS (Statistical Package for the Social Sciences) program. Qualitative research often relies on some form of thematic analysis with carefully laid out steps, usually based on established methods in the respective fields. Sometimes, researchers use NVivo, a well-known software, for this purpose. Here, the researchers will organise and present results of their analysis. Quantitative analysis typically requires the reporting of data on frequency, means, and significant differences between groups of participants.

These results are usually presented in tables or figures. Qualitative research usually presents the results in terms of themes.

Following the analysis, researchers will attempt to interpret the results in terms of the implications, explanations, strengths, limitations, as well as recommendations for future research. This stage is known as "Interpretation". The final stage is the "Conclusion". Here, the researchers reiterate their answers to the research question more directly and assert the significance of the research by highlighting the contribution to the field.

The entire research process is mirrored in the format that the research is written up. The sections in a research article are mainly the Introduction, Methodology, Results & Discussion and Conclusion. After the whole research manuscript is completed, the researchers will send the manuscript to an academic journal publisher for consideration. As you can see from the above research process, it is a very long and systematic process which requires planning and meticulousness. More precisely, the research process described here is known as "primary research". This means that the research is newly formulated by the researchers, conducted with original data sources and analyzed by the researchers themselves. In contrast, a research essay that is written based on previously published work and without any data collection can be termed "secondary research". This type of research essay is commonly assigned in undergraduate work. At the master and doctoral degree levels, primary research is emphasized more strongly.

Here, it is useful to understand what research is not. Writing a blog or posting a video about one's views on a particular issue in yoga is not research. Organizing a yoga nidra session and reporting on the event's happenings is not research. Reflecting about one's practice on the mat is usually not considered research although some research papers have provisions and space for a more reflective component. This reflection, however, has to be systematically documented and make connections with existing theories and concepts.

Research and Commercial Genres

At this juncture, let us turn our attention to understanding the various research and commercial genres that are used in academia and those are frequently seen in everyday life.

Ever since the invention of the printing press, knowledge has been disseminated widely. With the development of the Internet, it is now an understatement that the types of publications have increased exponentially. Even within each publication, there can be many different genres or text types. For example, a magazine may contain articles, advertisements, reflections, and opinion columns. Let's take a look at some genres that exist and see how a researcher usually thinks when perusing these various sources of information. If a researcher is conducting a research project and is going to write up a research article on it, which sources will he refer to and cite in this article? The following are some examples.

Handbook

A handbook surveys all the important topics and issues in a field or discipline. In this book, various authors who are experts in their field are invited to contribute a chapter. Examples of handbooks are the *Handbook of Complementary and Alternative Medicine* and the *Routledge Handbook of Yoga and Meditation Studies.*

Broadly speaking, a handbook on yoga may include topics on various traditions of yoga, new forms of yoga or yoga in therapy treatments, etc. Important concepts are covered, and significant research studies are cited. This provides a broad helicopter view of key topics in the field. As such, a handbook is usually a very thick book. Please note that in academic parlance, a 'handbook' is not an instructional or a 'how-to' manual. It does not teach a person how to do something step by step. Instead, an academic handbook is a comprehensive book which documents vital topics and concepts in the field.

Academic Book

Researchers may refer to academic books when doing research. This genre specifically refers to an academic book that is written by a scholar or commissioned by an editor. In the latter case, various authors are invited to write a chapter. However, the content of an academic book is usually not as extensive as a handbook. The academic book focuses on a specific topic and usually does not survey an entire field. Some examples are *Yoga: The Indian Tradition*, which is broad in scope or *Raja Yoga*, which focuses on a particular tradition of Yoga. Some graduates also publish their theses or dissertations as academic books if they are able to find a suitable publisher. The academic book, like the handbook, is a rich source of valuable knowledge about topics, ideas and concepts.

Academic Research Journal

The academic research journal publishes research conducted by scholars and researchers. Do note that the term 'journal' does not refer to diaries where entries are made every day, which is the meaning in popular media. In research, the periodical is a research publication produced on a regular basis (monthly, quarterly, half-yearly, annually, etc.). It contains original research articles, review articles and letters to the editors. The examples of academic journals referred to in this book are *BMC Complementary Medicine and Therapies*, *Evidence-Based Complementary and Alternative Medicine* and *BMC Complementary and Alternative Medicine*.

Historically, the research journal is the main means of communication among scientists, scholars and researchers. This form of disseminating research has continued till today and onward. Most breakthroughs in research in various fields are captured in academic journals. Most faculty members and researchers in universities and research institutes are required to conduct research and publish in academic journals. This then gets recognized and codified as knowledge, culminating in what is commonly known as knowledge creation. Research journals are published online and/or are available in hard copy, although it is now more common to see online journals because there is more online space, and it is more expedient to make research available.

It is important to understand the research publication process. The following description is typical of what happens although there may be some variations. Before a research article is published, it undergoes peer review. Let's say you are a yoga researcher who just completed your manuscript on 'Perceptions of yoga among senior citizens at a health center'. You identify an academic journal that publishes articles related to your research. For the purpose of this example, let's say you submit the article to a journal - Journal of Yoga Research. The editor receives your article and then sends it to two to three reviewers who are experts in this field. They will spend some time to review your manuscript and reply to you with comments. Some reviews take an extremely long time but usually not more than 6 months.

There are a few outcomes in this peer review process. They

are mainly 'accepted for publication without amendments', 'accepted for publication with amendments', and 'rejected for publication'. (The exact terminology varies across journals.) You receive the review result with reviewers' comments. The comments centre on content, arguments, organization and language. Most of the time, the article requires amendments, if accepted. As the author, you make the revisions and there may be one to two more rounds of reviews before the article is finalized for publication. This is to ensure a high content and language quality to the final document before the research becomes published.

This article that will eventually be published is known as the research article (RA). In this book, this is the genre that we will focus on. Sometimes, you may see the words 'original research' published alongside the article. As mentioned earlier, an academic journal also includes other texts such as 'Letter to the Editor' and 'Review Article'. However, research articles usually take up the majority of space in an academic journal more so than any other text.

In the sciences, a research article is usually authored by a team of researchers. Each research article cited in this book (see complete bibliography) is authored by a team of researchers. This teamwork ensures rigor in analysis and checks and balances in analysis, as well as ensures division of labor which enables a smooth execution of the entire research project.

Master Thesis or Doctoral Dissertation

Students enrolled in a master's degree by research or doctoral degree program usually submit a thesis or a dissertation by the end of their degree program. After the work is approved by the examination committee, the electronic and/

or hard copy version may be archived in the university library. This publication is usually not open to the public; however, a researcher may be able to request the publication through inter-institutional loans, in some instances.

Sometimes, a student may publish their doctoral dissertation as an academic book. In this case, it would be more judicious for researchers to refer to the book instead. However, most graduates do not publish their theses or dissertations. When researchers cite this work, they usually call it the 'Unpublished master's thesis or PhD dissertation'. Most researchers, however, will still prefer to cite academic research articles as they are more established.

Institutional Website

This category of sources includes university websites and government websites. A researcher may refer to these sources to refer to an official stance on a particular matter and/or their course of action on an issue. For instance, a Department of Health may express their position on a health product, medication, or an issue such as vaccination against COVID-19. You can get current information from an institutional website regarding an evolving situation but not fast enough from a research journal article, which takes months to years to be published.

Dictionary

Researchers will consult a dictionary to retrieve definitions of terms. Definitions are very important in research. The dictionaries in this category do not refer to the *Cambridge Dictionary, Merriam-Webster Dictionary* or *Collins Dictionary*. We are talking about academic or specialist dictionaries which focus on a subject or discipline. An example is the *Oxford Dictionary of Sport Science and Medicine*. It is important because these academic dictionaries are rigorously researched, and the definitions provided are more precise and may be different from everyday parlance.

The choice of words has a significant impact on building a common understanding among researchers. For example, a researcher may conduct a research project on investigating the efficacy of yoga school programs on students' well-being. In sampling the school programs, the researchers may scrutinise the programs in order to ascertain that they are indeed yoga programs before deciding to include them in the study. In order to do that, the researchers will need an official definition and/or description of yoga. In this case, they may consult an official source such as the Oxford Dictionary of Hinduism. It should be noted that the researcher may not use a definition from a common online English dictionary because researchers usually need more specific and precise descriptions.

With a clear definition, it is easier for researchers to compare and contrast their studies with those of others, so that meaningful conclusions can be drawn. Having said that, it is not uncommon to find that some research articles do not provide definitions of key terms they use in the article. This could be due to an oversight or the research community's familiarity with the terminology in the field. However, in any new or burgeoning field, information may not be readily available. If a specialized dictionary is not available, a researcher may then search for the next best source, perhaps a general dictionary or a reputable yoga website for the information.

Newspapers

Scientists usually do not refer to newspapers when conducting research studies. This is because the news is mainly for public consumption and is not meant for research. When a newspaper or online news network reports on a scientific breakthrough made by researchers, scientists usually will not use this source. Scientists will read the original research paper rather than the news article.

However, there may be times when a scientist refers to a newspaper when writing up their research. They may wish to quote someone who is cited in the newspapers. This might be unavailable in an academic journal. Perhaps, they may also want to refer to what happened at an event on a particular date. Lastly, some researchers may wish to draw attention to how some newspapers have covered a particular issue. Therefore, by and large, newspapers are not referred to by researchers for research information but for more specific purposes.

Commercial websites

In a similar vein, scientists are unlikely to prioritize commercial websites when citing information. Commercial websites on yoga can be yoga schools, yoga magazines, or yoga apparel companies. A researcher working on how yoga can improve mental well-being is unlikely to cite from any well-known online yoga magazines or medical news portals. This is also the case, even when the authors of the magazines are medical professionals with proper credentials.

The reason is that magazines have profit-driven objectives, and this may have some impact on the appearance of objectivity. For example, an online magazine can exclude or downplay how inversions could contribute to stress on practitioners' eyes. There may not be much discussion on detrimental or side effects of yoga in commercial websites. The articles on commercial websites generally do not undergo a rigorous peer review process. Therefore, a conflict of interest as well as a lack of rigorous peer review are likely to deter researchers from using information from commercial websites.

Summary

In summary, research then is systematic, formal and comprehensive, and rightfully so since the information is likely to be consumed by the professionals and public and applied in some way. The time needed is to ensure that all the facts, figures, and interpretation are properly reviewed before they go into publication. When conducting a research study, a researcher can refer to many possible sources. Research articles remain the first choice of reference followed by academic books and institutional websites. In the case of citing from non- academic sources, researchers usually will do so only in specific cases such as reporting of certain recent events or authorities' stance on an issue. In short, researchers are clear in knowing their exact purpose of citing from each source.

CHAPTER 2

RESEARCH ARTICLES - INTRODUCTION

A Note About the Research Article

Earlier, the academic research journal was introduced. Since many scientific breakthroughs are announced via the research article, this is the genre that we will cover in detail. It should be noted that other genres such as research reports and dissertations tend to follow this structure, although with some variations.

An academic research article usually adheres to the following structure:

- Introduction
- Data
- Methodology & Analytical Methods
- Results
- Discussion
- Conclusion

Sometimes, researchers call this the IMRDC structure.

As you read this chapter and the following chapters, it may be useful for you to download one of the research articles listed in the bibliography of this book. You will be able to see how the sections of an entire research article are organized.

Research writing is concerned with creating a coherent piece of writing that can communicate the study's findings and impact informatively and convincingly. Therefore, a research article contains many sections, each of which contains rhetorical elements or steps. The word "rhetorical" means to have a purpose.

Introduction

When reading a research article introduction, a reader is likely to be interested to know how the research study came about. For example, a research study may investigate the attitudes of yoga teachers toward chair yoga. A reader may ask some of the following questions.

Where does this research study take place, i.e., which country, city, institutions or yoga centers? Is chair yoga a widely practised form of yoga, and are formal chair yoga classes conducted at yoga centers at the research site? Is there any significance in studying this topic; that is, how does this study help with furthering the teaching and practice of yoga? For whom is the current study useful?

What is chair yoga and is there a standard definition? Is this yoga topic currently a topic of intense discussion or controversy? Is there a current lack of knowledge in this area of research? What do we already know about chair yoga in the research literature? Which field of yoga does chair yoga belong to and what are its origins and how did it develop through the years? More importantly, what is the research objective and the exact research questions that guide this study?

As you can see, some of the questions above relate to the research literature and others relate to the site of research. Bearing these points in mind, we will now examine some of the rhetorical steps in an Introduction. Do note that these are not covered in any particular order of importance.

Defining important terms

Researchers often offer definitions of key terms they use in a research study. Since yoga research is still in its nascent stages, most researchers do define it. Yoga has been referred to as:

> "an ancient tradition that incorporates postures, breathing techniques, meditation, and moral and ethical principles [1]" (Wang & Hagins, 2016, p. 1).

> "a gentle activity that combines physical movement (i.e., *asana*), breathing techniques (i.e., *pranayama*), and meditation (i.e., *dhyana*; [6])" (Mackenzie et al., 2016, p. 1).

As you can see from the foregoing definitions, they are mostly the same but slightly different. Providing definitions is important for two reasons. Firstly, definitions in academic texts are meant to be precise and they may differ from how general audiences understand a term. For instance, the thing that comes to mind in the popular arena when someone mentions yoga, is that it comprises mainly physical postures (asanas). However, that is not how academic texts or experienced yoga teachers define yoga as it has other elements. Secondly and more importantly, definitions give the reader an appropriate point of reference so that they know the boundaries of the term. For instance, this definition may not include new types of yoga that have been recently conceived.

However, do note that some researchers do not provide definitions of certain key terms in their research. It is possible that they think the specialist reader would know what they are saying. However, sometimes, this can be counterproductive. For instance, if the focus of research article is about "diaphragmatic breathing", a definition should be provided. Not very researcher will be well-versed in a subfield or know every single term from memory. Definitions are thus usually included in the Introduction.

Introducing the research topic within a context

Research does not occur in a vacuum. One of the important rhetorical steps that researchers follow is to start more generally in a research article before focusing on the topic. For instance, a research study may wish to examine yoga participants' attitudes toward chair and desk yoga. It is important to situate the context appropriately in the context. For instance, researchers may draw attention to the increasing level of stress at the workplace, especially among office workers due to the long hours. Sometimes, exercise may not be a regular option for many of these workers. Chair and desk yoga will fit into this picture well. Notice that this topic may also fit in contexts such as senior citizen centers or even schools. However, researchers may only focus on the workplace as more and more corporations are looking toward offering yoga classes as part of their learning and development programs.

Notice how locating their research in context can be done

by researchers. In their exploratory research, Mackenzie et al., (2016) examined cancer survivors' experiences in a yoga program. Notice the general framework at the beginning of the study:

> "Approximately 1.9 million individuals are diagnosed with cancer each year in North America [1] ... Cancer is amongst the leading cause of morbidity and mortality in North America [3] ... (p. 1).

The authors continue to bring up the negative psychosocial impact of cancer and mention how cancer patients peruse coping methods to mitigate cancer and treatment effects, before mentioning Yoga:

> "Yoga has emerged as one such self-management strategy." (p. 1)

As can be seen from the abovementioned text, the authors first provide some background information about the number of patients with cancer. No information was mentioned about yoga yet. After about three sentences later, the topic of yoga was then brought up to show the link. This sets up the topic in terms of its relevance and interest.

In this regard, research writing is different from most popular genres of writing such as news articles which typically mentions the most important information first. Journalistic pieces are usually shorter pieces and has little turnaround time. Research articles tend to be more comprehensive; therefore, they provide more background information, thus allowing the reader to get a fuller understanding of the topic.

Reviewing past research

In an Introduction, you are very likely to read about some past research on the topic specifically. This is not merely for historical documentation but sets up a meaningful discussion about what has been done or how the topic has developed over the years.

If researchers wish to study senior citizens' opinions of chair yoga, they will first read past journal articles and books for related research. This may include reading research on senior citizens' exercise regimes, motivations for attending yoga classes, efficacy of chair yoga classes on physical, mental and emotional health. There may also be studies that have covered elderly's attitude toward chair yoga or other forms of assistive yoga. These researchers would want to know how their own study can continue the academic conversation on this topic. Perhaps they may wish to examine this topic from another new angle, perspective or include new variables.

In the introductory section of their qualitative research of how urban school students regarded the advantages of yoga, Wang and Hagins (2016) highlighted two previous related qualitative studies,

> "a 12-week yoga program helped students with their athletic performance, bodily awareness, academic performance, sleep, and mental health ..." (p. 1).

> "an 8-week yoga-based program helped third grade students to feel calm and focused, provided strategies to help control emotions, and supported positive self-esteem ..." (p. 1).

Reviewing past literature is important. First, it is the responsibility of researchers to survey what has already been published on the topic. Second, they usually need to distinguish the current study from past research so that they can extend an understanding of the topic. If all researchers are working on the exact same old samples and research questions all the time, it would be difficult to advance the field with new insights.

[Note: Sometimes, this review of past research becomes an entire section on its own called 'Literature Review" or "Review of Literature", depending on the journal's editorial direction.]

After reviewing the research, researchers usually critique the research by reviewing briefly the positive and negative aspects of the research. However, remarks about what is insufficient or flawed in the research sets up a space for the researchers to surface a research gap:

> "Given the above, there is currently **a lack of published qualitative studies** providing information directly from student voices." (Wang & Hagins, 2016, p. 1, emphasis mine)

This is usually signposted using some form of negative criticism. In the above research study, the researchers cited the only two qualitative studies known to exist on this topic, implying that there have been insufficient qualitative studies.

A research gap can be conveyed in various ways. For instance, there might be no study on a particular population or group of people. There may be yoga studies on cancer patients but there are no such studies on people suffering from severe depression. Another possibility is that there is no research on the topic at all. Although this is very unlikely, it could happen if the topic or phenomenon is extremely new, e.g., COVID-19 in its early stages. In terms of yoga, a researcher may find that there are no existing studies on rope wall yoga. One of the frequent questions I get from students is: What happens if the topic has never been investigated. How do we review the literature then? My response is that there is past research on yoga, and perhaps, the students can search for studies that examine forms of yoga that involve props. Research articles on exercises involving rope and wall exercises are likely to exist. These publications can be reviewed before establishing the research gap. Having said that, I would also encourage researchers to do a thorough search of the research literature to make sure there is indeed no existing study on this topic before claiming it to be so. A quick search on the Internet reveals that there is research on less well-known yoga practices such as chair yoga, aerial yoga, and laughter yoga.

Emphasizing the value of the study

If you read a research article, you are likely to question its value: what is the significance of this study? What is the point? For instance, if I come across an article on perceptions of yoga nidra on anxiety and sleep management, I might wonder if this is a significant topic worthy of research. Is this currently a topic of intense debate, thus warranting attention? Are many people now suffering from anxiety and insomnia? Are the insights derived from this study going to be useful for these groups of people? Is this survey study going to be representative of the population for which it intends to generalize? Will this study generate more in-depth understanding of the topic?

In this regard, besides establishing the research gap, a study usually emphasizes the significance of the study. Consider the following example:

"Unlike previous qualitative assessments of yoga programs in schools, the current study incorporated focus groups from several different schools, was based on a year-long yoga program, and was primarily comprised of minority youth." (Wang & Hagins, 2016, p. 2).

This statement signalled that the study distinguished itself from preceding research in terms of scale, duration and specific population, establishing its value and contribution to the field. Bear in mind that researchers value originality and normally do not want to publish the same research as other researchers. More significantly, establishing a research gap is usually not sufficient to warrant carrying out a new study. For instance, if there is no research currently on rope wall yoga, this does not necessarily mean that researchers will carry out a study on this topic. A justification solely via a research gap is not persuasive enough. There must be sufficient interest and a strong rationale to conduct a study like this. In addition, arguing for the significance of a study can be rather subjective; therefore, it is usually up to the researchers to make a case for uniqueness or originality.

Research objective/questions

One of the key rhetorical steps in a research article introduction is stating the research objective(s) or research question(s), usually at the end of the section. The research objective fills the gap in the research study. In fact, this is one of the first few statements that an experienced reader may focus on when reading the introduction. However, do note that it is also quite rare for a research article to state the research objective in the first paragraph of the introduction. In this book, the term 'research objective' is used interchangeably with 'research goal' or 'research aim'.

The following are examples of research questions:

> "The overall guiding research questions were as follows: Do urban youth perceive benefits from learning and practicing yoga? And if so, in what specific ways." (Wang & Hagins, 2016, p. 2)

From the above, it is evident that the research gap usually leads logically to the research questions/research objectives. The research questions guide the entire study, and the researchers will answer this question at the end of the study. The research question does not mean that this is the only question that participants will be asked during the research. Most objectives/questions and phenomena are complex and multifaceted. Hence, a research question can be examined further with more specific questions in the survey questionnaire.

In some studies, research questions are not included. A research objective is included instead. This usually means that it is phrased as a statement rather than a question. An example is as follows:

> "Therefore, the aim of this study was to assess the acceptability and feasibility of the intervention, by exploring service users' experiences of Yoga4Health, and facilitators and barriers to participation and continued yoga practice." (Cheshire et al., 2022, p. 3)

This statement is very clear in highlighting the two key concerns 'acceptability and feasibility' and examining aspects such as 'users' experiences, facilitators and barriers'. There are no research questions following it.

Researchers may sometimes use a combination of research objective and research questions in the introduction. For instance, if the research objective of a study is to examine the attitudes of yoga teachers toward various styles of yoga, it is possible to state the Research Questions as follows:

Research Question 1: What do experienced yoga teachers think about vinyasa yoga?

Research Question 2: What do experienced yoga teachers think about rope wall yoga?

Research Question 3: What do experienced yoga teachers think about aerial yoga?

Stating the research questions directly sometimes can allow the researchers to address every question in a more organized and clearer manner. Sometimes, however, researchers avoid providing both research objective and research questions because they may sound repetitive.

At this juncture, it would be timely for us to take a look the titles of research articles. In most articles, titles are meant to be attention-grabbing and informative. Some titles are more concise than others, but it depends on the individual journal's editorial direction. Consider some of the following titles:

- "I wouldn't have joined if it wasn't online": Understanding older people's engagement with teleyoga classes for fall prevention (Haynes et al., 2022)
- Yoga in adult cancer: An exploratory, qualitative analysis of the patient experience (McCall et al., 2015)
- Perceived benefits of yoga among urban school students: A qualitative analysis (Wang & Hagins, 2016)

Titles of research articles are usually well thought out by researchers. Evident from the titles above, the **main topics** are captured concisely: teleyoga, yoga in adult cancer, and perceived benefits of yoga, respectively. Moreover, the sample group of participants are also mentioned, namely, older people, patients, urban school students, respectively. The second and third example even highlight the **qualitative** orientation of the research. This possibly distinguishes the research from much research that tends to be more quantitative, which tends to produce fewer rich data. In addition, it is not uncommon to include a quote from a participant in a research article title. This is usually done to highlight a key point or interesting finding which generates interest in the research study.

As a consumer of researcher, as you read a research article, the article title and the research objective should guide and help you re-focus your understanding of the study. In fact, the title can be thought of as a mini research objective or mini thesis statement which serves as a spinal column for the entire research article.

Reading with discernment

Now that you have learned the moves of the Introduction, perhaps some questions are running through your mind. You might feel that you disagree with something mentioned in the article, and that is perfectly normal. This is because readers of research tend to evaluate the logic and ideas of what they read. This means that you are reading the text with a critical eye.

Here are some potential questions that could assist you to form your ideas and opinions as you are reading the Introduction. Is the title clearly expressed? Do you get a clear idea of what the topic is about? Does the aim of the research study align with the article title? Does the study make a successful case for its significance or uniqueness? Is a definition or clarifying phrase provided for the key term used in the study? Are there any ambiguous terms? Is a gap in the existing research identified through sufficient perusal of past related studies? Do the researchers give sufficient information on the research site, that is, about where they are conducting the research? Do the research questions state clearly what the study wishes to investigate?

These questions are not exhaustive, and they can serve to guide you as you read the introductory section of the research article. A useful approach is also reading the research article first on your own, and then using these questions as a supplement.

Summary

The Introduction covers the background of the research study, emphasizes its significance, reviews past research literature, establishes the gap in research and provides the research goal and questions. These elements with their rhetorical steps lead logically to the next section, which describes the methodology of data collection and analytical methods.

CHAPTER 3

RESEARCH ARTICLES
– METHODOLOGY

In the Methodology section, the researchers describe the methods through which they collect and analyze their data. It is important to convey that the research data was collected ethically, and the methodological design is robust, rigorous, and systematic. As a reader, I may be wondering how the research participants were recruited, how the research study was executed, how the data was collated, and which analytical method was chosen. More importantly, I may want to see if the methodology ties in well with the research questions from the Introduction.

For instance, if a research study chooses to examine the opinions of yoga practitioners toward hatha, yin, restorative yoga in multiple yoga centers, I would probably expect a survey questionnaire to be used. I would also expect it to include many more items than that of a smaller-scale study. I may also wonder if any sampling method was employed to form the final sample of yoga centers and research participants. This is important because it potentially affects the representativeness of the results, if the researchers have this goal in mind. For a large-scale study, I would not expect researchers to collect data via focus groups since there are numerous participants. I would definitely not expect the research to conduct a clinical experiment as the latter is not used for gathering opinions.

Conversely, if a research study examines the efficacy of specific yogic breathing techniques on concentration, I would probably expect an experiment setup. After the session(s) on yogic breathing are conducted, the group of participants may be asked to partake in a specially designed psychomotor test that measures accuracy and speed. These results can be recorded with precise instruments. In this regard, I would not expect a research study to only use survey questionnaires because that is based predominantly on self-reports. These, however, can be used as a supplementary instrument if the researchers are interested in examining what the respondents think or feel about their concentration ability.

Researchers have the option to use mixed methods, that is, combining both quantitative and qualitative methods, although a number of studies align with one of the orientations. Whichever method is employed by the researcher, a reader would be interested in the credibility and rigor of the method. In addition, as most yoga research involves human subjects, a reader would expect to be informed about the ethics clearance. With the foregoing examples in mind, let us turn our attention to the various rhetorical steps covered in a Methodology section of a research article.

Ethical consideration

In the vast majority of studies, researchers are required to seek ethical clearance in order to conduct research. In many developed countries with an active research milieu, the norm is to submit the proposal to an ethics review institution before data collection is allowed. This is meant to protect the participants from any potential harm that might result from the study. This is especially crucial if participants are receiving a particular treatment that involves chemicals or undergoing a program that may potentially contribute to side effects. Here is a declaration of an ethically approved research:

> "Ethical approval was obtained from a Research Ethics Board (REB) and all participants completed an REB-approved informed consent prior to study enrollment." (Mackenzie et al., 2016, p. 2)

Before the researchers can start interviewing the participants, they need to receive a completed informed consent form from the participants. This form usually communicates the research study purpose, intervention or program that participants will undergo, the benefits and potential dangers that may occur, confidentiality of the information, contact information of researchers, and the participants' right to withdraw from the program at any stage of the research. It is important to convey to participants that research participation is voluntary. Furthermore, participants are usually promised 'confidentiality' for their response. For example, in qualitative research, responses from the participants can be reported verbatim or in chart analysis, but they are never attributed by name to avoid identification. Names of participants are not mentioned in the research, which explains why confidentiality, not anonymity, is guaranteed. In some research, for example, a particular school, center or institute, is not even made known in the study.

Some have even queried – what kind of harm can come to a person through survey questionnaires or a non-kinesthetic form of intervention? The response is we can never be sure about the triggers that various people may have when encountering questions. There is a possibility that questions or stimulus can evoke unfavorable reactions, especially sensitive topics such as disease and trauma. Therefore, it is imperative to be respectful to all participants and to adopt a more circumspect approach.

Recruitment and Sampling Method

In order to collect the required data successfully, the recruitment process and sampling of participants are usually carefully planned. There are many ways of recruitment such as going through official administration channels, word-of-mouth, advertisements on campus noticeboards, letters to patients, etc., as well as many sampling methods such as random sampling, systematic sampling, snowball sampling, etc. For instance, if I am conducting a study on senior citizens' opinions of chair yoga, I have some criteria in my recruitment and sampling. For instance, I may first use a random sampling method to sample the senior citizen centers or rehabilitation centers, followed by recruitment through chair yoga sessions conducted at these centers. I may also have a set of criteria such as a minimum number of hours of chair yoga sessions that participants have attended. Indeed, there are a variety of sampling methods that are available to researchers. What is important is that it suits the researchers' purpose.

In their study of cancer patients' experience of yoga, McCall et al. (2015) describe the recruitment as follows:

> "English-speaking patients receiving conventional treatment in Vancouver, Canada were recruited for this study through poster

advertisements in two cancer hospitals and three complementary care clinics." (p. 2)

The researchers were rather meticulous in mentioning the language and the venues through which the participants were enlisted. In the next section, they provided information on their sampling method. They utilized purposive sampling which is based on a set of criteria such as "age, gender, characteristics of disease and therapeutic use of yoga and other complementary therapies during cancer treatment" (p. 2).

Sampling is necessary because it is impossible to interview everyone, and therefore, only a certain percentage of people would be interviewed. It is important to remember that all research studies have logistical constraints. There are also other available sampling methods, but they may not suit the researchers' purpose. For instance, if they had utilized convenience sampling, the final group of participants might have included participants who were non-English speaking. You might also notice here that the names of the hospitals and cancer care are not mentioned. This is because most of the data collated here can be sensitive information, and withholding this information aims to protect the privacy of the participants. Some research studies may refer to the institution using generic descriptions such as "large public school" or "in the suburban area".

Purposive sampling, snowball sampling and convenience sampling

In the abovementioned study, the sampling method used was purposive sampling. As the name suggests, purposive sampling is employed with specific criteria in mind. At the hospitals, the researchers did not recruit people who did not use yoga or complementary therapies because that would not yield data that address the research objectives and in-depth interview questions. Purposive sampling enables the researchers to reach out to specific groups of people. Sometimes, another method known as snowball sampling may be used by researchers, especially if it is difficult to recruit some participants. For example, researchers may wish to interview respondents with an extremely rare ailment. They may ask their only participant to refer them to other possible interviewees as they may be in the same support group for the rare ailment.

Apart from purposive and snowball sampling, another method known as 'convenience sampling' is less frequently used. This means the researchers may recruit people they know or anyone who is within their vicinity of the research. The drawback of this method is that it is not rigorous at all. If the aim of the study is to generalize findings to an entire population of yoga practitioners in a city or a country, it would make little sense for a researcher to reach out to anyone whom they know as the results will not be representative. Instead, for such studies, researchers often prefer to employ more rigorous methods of sampling such as random sampling, stratified sampling and systematic sampling, to which we now turn.

Let's use a simple example to understand these sampling methods.

Suppose you are a researcher. You wish to conduct a qualitative study to investigate Grade 12 students' attitude toward yoga lessons. You will recruit the participants to form a focus group. You don't want to conduct a quantitative survey because you are more interested in understanding the participants' perceptions in greater depth. It would be impossible to ask all Grade 12 students in a focus group, that is, assuming that you only have the resources to conduct one focus group consisting of 10 students. The following are some options for more rigorous sampling to ensure a better representation of the population.

Random sampling

The first step is to obtain a complete list of names of students and number them sequentially from 1 to 100. There should not be any repeated numbers. Using a random number generation function in an Excel Spreadsheet, you can generate 10 random numbers. For instance, the numbers may be 2, 9, 14, 22, 37, 44, 51, 78, 91, and 94. The students whose names correspond with these numbers will be selected to form this focus group. The rationale for using this method is that each student should have a fair and equal chance of getting picked. Please note that random sampling is **not** convenience sampling. The latter does not involve steps in minimizing bias.

Stratified sampling

Another option that researchers have is to use stratified sampling. Assuming that final sample as a result of random sampling consists of 8 female students and 2 male students. Although the sampling is conducted fairly, you hope that the voices of both genders are more equally represented in this research.

In this regard, you create a list consisting of female students (List A), and another list consisting of male students (List B). Hence, gender is the criterion used for stratification. From here, you generate 5 random numbers for List A and List B respectively. The names corresponding to the numbers will be in the final sample of 10 students.

Of course, gender is not the only variable that a researcher may consider for stratified sampling. Variables such as prior experience with yoga practices, socioeconomic status (SES), income level can be used as the variable for stratification as well. It all depends on the research questions and the need to mitigate potential bias.

Systematic sampling

At times, researchers may use systematic sampling as random sampling may not be ideal. Using the foregoing example, researchers may find most of the random numbers generated might unexpectedly turn up within the range of 20. Therefore, they may want to avoid any potential bias caused by this number cluster.

To ensure a good spread throughout the sample, the researchers may choose to sample every 9th student name on the list until they obtain the final sample of 10 students. Sometimes, researchers may combine both systematic and stratified sampling. Whichever sampling method the researchers choose, they need to provide a good reason for choosing it.

Procedures

One important rhetorical step is describing the procedures of the research study; that is, how the research was carried out. If it is a survey study, it is important to know how the surveys were administered to the respondents. Were they sent via email or given out in person? How much time were the respondents given to complete the survey? If it is a qualitative study involving in-depth interviews, did the researchers have to follow a specific script or a list of semi-structured questions? What is the duration of each interview? When do the interviewers actually end the interview? Who were the interviewers and were they trained to conduct the interview? As you can see, these are some of the information that researchers may include in the research study. Notice how the following study describes the manner in which the research was conducted:

> "The focus groups lasted approximately 20-40 minutes and were all conducted by one person, who was not affiliated with the yoga study in any other way. Due to school regulations, the focus groups were not audio-recorded but instead had two research assistants take notes throughout. Upon completion of each focus group, each research assistant transcribed and reviewed the notes and sent them to the interviewer for review." (Wang & Hagins, 2016, p. 2)

The description is fairly detailed above, giving information on time and even mentioning that the person is an outsider of the research. This likely bolsters the credibility of the study as it minimizes bias. In research, if researchers are the participants' yoga teachers, this can induce an unwanted effect where participants may attempt to impress the teacher. In addition, participants may provide socially desirable answers so as not to diminish their stature. The study was also very transparent in mentioning that the notes, instead of audio, were captured during the focus groups. The interviewer's perusal of the notes also ensured the rigor and quality of the method. Taken together, a meticulously described procedure conveys trustworthiness of the data collected which will be analyzed for results.

Instruments

Researchers often describe the materials and instruments that they are using to collect the data. In an experiment setup, there is usually a control group and an experimental group. If researchers are interested in examining the impact of yoga intervention on concentration, then the experimental group will likely undergo the yoga intervention. Following that, the researchers may administer a psychomotor task to assess the participants' performance and compare it with the group without the yoga intervention. The psychomotor task may involve using a touchscreen, which is the instrument in this case. In this regard, the microscope, thermometer, MRI machine can all be considered instruments if they are used in a research study.

In a survey study, the instrument is the survey questionnaire which contains a battery of questions. In a focus group interview, the list of interview questions is considered the instrument. This list is sometimes called an interview script.

Consider the following study conducted by Mackenzie et al. (2016) in which the instrument used was the list of interview questions. The article was comprehensive in providing two interview scripts used at different stages of the study. Examples of questions are:

> "(1)(xi) What role does yoga play in your cancer recovery?" (p.3)

> "(2)(v) When people don't practice yoga as often as they'd like, why not?" (p. 3)

In the above study, questions included in the interview script align closely with the research objective in the introduction, which is to examine "cancer survivors and their support persons' experiences following a seven-week community-based yoga program" (Mackenzie et all., 2016, p. 2). Generally, all research studies carefully maintain this type of coherence from the research objective to the specific parts (e.g., focus group questions) of the study. This is because the responses collected will accrue and help the researchers answer the research question with a detailed answer. In some research articles, you will be able to locate the survey questionnaire at the end of the article under a header called "Appendix". In such cases, the researchers usually describe the content types of questions that are being asked and give the respective examples. The reader is asked to refer to the Appendix for more information. However, some research articles do not provide the entire questionnaire anywhere in the article.

Method of Analysis

Now imagine that you have gathered a lot of data, how are you going to analyze them? If the data is quantitative the researchers usually analyze them using descriptive and inferential statistics. Suffice to note that, in terms of descriptive statistics, researchers will normally tabulate and calculate the frequency and mean (average) of the certain variable. As for inferential statistics, they will run tests such as T-tests, Analysis of Variance (ANOVA) or Multivariate Analysis of Variance (MANOVA) to see if there are any significant differences between groups of participants.

What if the data is qualitative, i.e., they are transcriptions of participants' responses during interviews or focus groups? How do they analyze paragraphs and paragraphs of words? They usually use a method of analysis that has been established by past research. Notice how the transcripts from the focus groups were analyzed.

> "As suggested by Miles and Huberman [10], analysis began with a list of preliminary codes based on the theory and existing literature.... Transcripts read by the interviewer were initially analyzed using open coding with key phrases noted. After this was completed, based on constant comparative method (CCM) that examines contrasts across respondents, situations, and settings [12], key words and phrases were compared and contrasted and grouped together to form themes in response to the questions that were asked. The contents (or phrases from the focus groups) were then given particular themes." (Wang & Hagins, 2016, p. 2)

It is evident that the above textual analysis was rigorous. The initial analysis which started with initial codes as well as the CCM are both established in past research as denoted by the citations [10] and [12]. In research, a top-down approach of data analysis refers to beginning with a set of pre-determined themes and then marking up the data according to them. Evident from the above, these themes were not random but derived from theory and literature. On the other hand, a bottom-up approach starts with the data at hand without any preconceived themes. Typically, a researcher reads the text with an open mind and marks up the data accordingly after many rounds of reading. By employing a top-down approach with the "preliminary codes" (p. 2) and bottom-up approach with the "open coding" (p. 2) in data analysis, the study conveys that the analysis is comprehensive. Moreover, comparison, contrast and grouping of text suggests there is cross-checking and shuttling between texts to ensure accuracy and fairness in analysis. Analytical processes and their detailed descriptions, such as these, are important in demonstrating the credibility of the study. This also counters potential questions of browsing or cherry-picking the text. Taken together, the text rhetorically conveys that the methodology used is trustworthy and persuasive, and never impressionistic.

There are other ways of analyzing qualitative data and researchers usually pick the one that suits their study best. Consider a different analytical method below used in the interview study of cancer patients by McCall et al. (2015) which highlighted that they used "interpretive description [17, 18]" (p. 2), "Qualitative Analysis Guide of Leuven (QUAGOL) (MM) [20]" (p. 2).

The citations indicated by numbers in the square parentheses indicate that these analytical methods exist in the research literature. They go on to provide a brief description of the analytic process which employed "an iterative process of constant comparison methods [21] to identity emergent patterns (MM, ST)" (p. 2). Analysis in research therefore is systematic and never sporadic. It is also useful to note that the letters in parentheses represented the name initials of the researchers who took charge of the respective stages of data analysis. This transparency of task allocation instills accountability and confidence in the research study.

Justification for Choices

Researchers normally justify their use of certain methods to bolster the credibility of the study. For example, if researchers conduct a survey study, they may use or adapt a questionnaire that has been used in another study. They might explain that it is a well-established method that has been used in research. If modifications are made to the surveys, researchers may explain why these changes are necessary for the participants they were interviewing. In addition, imagine a scenario for a qualitative study where hours and hours of audio recordings are converted to numerous pages of typewritten transcripts. Typically, researchers will derive various themes and subthemes using a systematic method of analysis as well as software tools. Consider the following example of a study where focus group discussions were conducted:

> "All focus groups were transcribed verbatim and analyzed using the NVivo 9 computer program (QSR International, 2010). The program allows for the organization of textual data into categories, themes, and subthemes and facilitates management of a large volume of textual data." (Mackenzie et al., 2016, p. 3)

Notice that the researchers did not merely stop at naming the program and then carried on with more description of the analytical method. Instead, they briefly described the key functions of the program to give the reader an idea of how it facilitates the analysis of a huge amount of data. This rhetorical step is important especially for researchers who are less familiar with qualitative research. In addition, NVivo is a well-known program in the field of qualitative analysis, which further bolsters the credibility of the study. Furthermore, justifications address potential questions as to why a particular program or analytical method is the most preferred one among others.

Moreover, researchers may sometimes justify their choice

of certain sampling approaches. For instance, McCall et al. (2015) stated that:

> "The sample size parameters were set to meet resource limitations and quality standards and included minimum 10 hours of interview time collected from a patient sample size minimum (n = 8) and maximum (n = 20)." (p. 2)

As you can see, the interview duration and sample size parameters potentially help answer potential questions a reader may have: when do researchers decide to end the interviews? When does the study consider to have interviewed an appropriate number of patients in the sample? The researchers pointed to the factors of resources and quality. These details are also indicative of a carefully thought-out research design which ensures the collection of sufficient data. Notice that in a Methodology section, many details are given. This is important as future researchers may wish to replicate the study or base their study on the current one. In addition, even though the methodology is ostensibly descriptive, the justification for various methodological or analytical decisions as well as detailed description confer upon it a persuasive orientation.

In short, where relevant, the methodology describes the following features:

- Participants – who are the people involved in the study? (o.g., working adults, cancer patients, high school students)
- Method of recruitment – how are the participants recruited for this study? (e.g., poster ad, on-site recruitment, email?)

- Sampling method – how are participants selected? (e.g., random sampling, convenience sampling, snowball sampling, systematic sampling?)
- Instrument – Is there a survey questionnaire? Is there a battery of test questions that participants are required to complete? What is the equipment used to measure the participants' response? What stimuli is provided to elicit the response of the participants?
- What is the method of data collection? (e.g., audio transcription, collation via spreadsheets, transcription?) Does it follow any established protocol?
- What is the method of analysis? (e.g., descriptive/ inferential statistics, grounded approach, thematic analysis, software such as SPSS or NVivo?)

Reading with discernment

As you are reading the article, you might be wondering why the researchers choose a particular method. Perhaps you have another method in mind. Here may be some questions that you have in mind. Is the overall research well designed? Are the stimuli and instruments e.g., survey questionnaire, semi-structured question list, written test described clearly? Is the method chosen a logical and appropriate choice based on the research questions? Is the sampling method an appropriate method? Do the researchers use the appropriate analytical methods? Is the data collection process sound? Is the method of analysis an established one? If not, do the researchers justify their analytical approach?

Summary

In a Methodology section, the researchers typically describe the participants, materials, instruments, method of recruitment and data collection, sampling method, and analytical method and provide justification for various decisions. With a sound research design, they are then able to collate data that are meaningful and useful. The next chapter covers the 'Results & Discussion'.

CHAPTER 4

RESEARCH ARTICLES – RESULTS & DISCUSSION

The Results & Discussion section is arguably the most significant section of a research study. It is here that findings and useful insights are presented and discussed, pushing the boundaries of knowledge about the topic and phenomenon. The 'Results' section is sometimes called 'Findings'. The findings may be combined with the discussion section to form a 'Results & Discussion' section. However, in some research studies, they are in separate sections.

Presenting results is not as easy as it looks because it needs to be done in an organized manner. For instance, if researchers conduct a quantitative study on university undergraduates' attitudes toward a yoga program, questions can be asked about the 'quality' and 'engagement' aspects of the program. Let's say, these questions are asked on a 5-point scale consisting of: 'Strongly disagree', 'Agree', 'Neither agree nor disagree', 'Agree' and 'Strongly agree'. Participants are required to indicate their degree of agreement in response to statements like these:

Quality Questions

Q1: The learning materials contain relevant written examples.

Q2: The learning materials contain relevant practice exercises.

Q3: The instructor is knowledgeable about the topics.

Engagement Questions

Q4: The instructor presents the topics in an interactive manner.

Q5: The instructor allocates tasks that require collaboration such as pair discussion and group presentations.

Q6: The instructor allocates time for asking questions and clarifying doubts.

In this regard, the researcher may present all the statistics related to 'Quality' first and then go on to present those of 'Engagement' either in prose or tables and figures. Taken together, these relate to the concept of 'attitudes toward the yoga program'. There may be many other questions in the survey questionnaire. Of course, researchers may choose to highlight only a few key questions in the reporting of results and then collate the complete set of numbers and percentages in tables and figures.

More importantly, the researcher must have a system for presenting the results as clearly as possible. With this simple example in mind, let's look at the various rhetorical steps in a 'Results' section. These steps are not presented in a particular order of importance. However, it is logical that researchers present some facts and figures before referring to tables and figures.

Results

Reporting an overview of results

Most research studies begin presenting the results by providing some general information such as the profile of the participants. This is important as it gives the reader a general idea of the scale of the study and enables them to read the subsequent results in context. Haynes et al. (2022) in their study of participants' views on an online yoga program, reported that:

> "Twelve SAGE participants took part in focus groups ... Of the 12 focus group participants, nine were women, six lived in urban areas and six in regional or rural areas, four of which had low income status." (p. 4)

The participants' profile gives us an idea of the diverse background and provides some assurance of heterogeneity of views so that a rich amount of useful data can be collated. The researchers went on to give some demographic information about the Yoga instructors that were also involved in this research. You may notice that these details are usually not included under 'sampling' in the 'Methodology' section because the researchers have set out to recruit may not result in the exact numbers. For instance, a few participants may pull out in the middle of the research study; therefore, the final sample size may not be what was planned. The final sample size may lean toward a certain demographic such as ethnicity or income status.

Compare this with another study by Cramer et al. (2019) who conducted a large online national survey. The 'Results' section began with some brief information:

"A total of 1702 participants completed the online survey. Sociodemographic and yoga practice characteristics of participants are presented in Table 1 and Table 2, respectively."
(p. 3)

In the tables, the researchers provided the profiles of the respondents with a breakdown according to variables such as age, gender, education, marital status, employment status, main yoga style, practice location, etc. As the researchers provided a lot of details, it is more organized to present them in the table format. In smaller-scale studies, the researchers would allocate one to two paragraphs on providing the overview.

When the research involves a survey, the researchers usually report the total number of admissible surveys. Sometimes, researchers report the response rate (in percentage). This means that they calculate the percentage of return responses out of the disseminated surveys. The response rate for hard copy surveys is generally lower than that of electronic surveys as respondents are less inclined to reply using the self-addressed envelope. Most surveys today are electronic and there is also a good reason for this. It is much easier to export the data into the Excel Spreadsheet or other formats so that it is easy to perform calculations or statistical tests. When the surveys are collated, the researchers will check through the results to make sure that they can be used. The researchers may also provide the reasons for discarding certain surveys such as incomplete information or invalid responses.

In short, a general breakdown of the respondents' profile and participation rate is usually given so that it is easier for the reader to understand the specific findings in context.

Presenting the main findings

This rhetorical step move is arguably the most important in this section. Bear in mind that the research is not impressionistic but is based on evidence. In this regard, detailed evidence in the form of results are provided. In a quantitative study, the researchers usually present some figures as a result of calculation or statistical analysis whereas in a qualitative study, themes are usually reported.

For instance, Cramer et al. (2019) stated:

> "Out of 1702 participants who completed the survey, 364 (21.4%) reported a total of 702 acute adverse effects." (p. 3)

In this instance, both the exact figures and percentages are given. Researchers usually endeavor to be as precise as possible in their reporting. However, researchers may not include in the main write-up, the figures for each question asked in the survey. Some may only discuss the key questions from the survey. If the long survey contains thirty or more questions, it can become unwieldy to discuss all the questions in words. Instead, some researchers may provide this information in tables or figures, and then consolidate the main insights.

In a qualitative study, the results are presented somewhat differently. Most qualitative studies present the results in terms of themes. The themes are usually derived based on an established process of analyzing and cross-checking the data set. In this study, there were four main themes related to mental benefits and 2 related to physical benefits, and one related to challenges.

For instance, Wang and Hagins (2016) reported a theme,

"*4.3 Stress Reduction*" (p. 3). Under this heading, they described:

> "Participants articulated how yoga helped them to relax and reduce stress. Often, they discussed how the yoga class was the only place they could do so during the course of the day." (p. 3)

This insight was further elaborated upon and subsequently supported with some data verbatim such as the following:

> "I like it (the yoga) – I am a fast person, being loud – yoga helps me step out of that and relax ... put my phone down and relax." (p. 3)

Providing some examples of the data verbatim is important as it helps the reader to see how the data build up to form the theme.

In forming themes, researchers are usually very careful to provide themes that are distinct from one another. Consider a scenario where if researchers present the themes "Yoga gives me energy" and "Yoga gives me physical and mental strength". One can argue that the words energy and strength are fairly synonymous in certain respects. Although the data can help clarify the difference in the meaning of the themes, it is still crucial that the themes provided avoid overlaps in broad meaning.

As you can see, the rhetorical step taken here by the researchers is predominantly reporting information as revealed by calculation and thematic analysis. The information is very specific and based on evidence from the data.

Providing general remarks

Sometimes, researchers do offer brief comments about specific findings although they do not comment on every result. They may wish to highlight a finding that is rather interesting, serendipitous, or noteworthy. These comments are usually short and span about one to a few sentences. For instance, Cheshire et al. (2022) reported how a few participants remarked about the usefulness of breathing exercises and how one participant opined that they caused her anxiety to worsen (pp. 6-7). Based on these responses, the researchers remarked:

> "These comments highlight the divergent experiences of some participants with existing mental health conditions." (p. 7)

When making comments in the 'Results' section, researchers generally do not go into great detail. There could be a few reasons for this approach. First, this forms part of all the findings. The researchers can consolidate all the results in this section so that the reader can obtain a fuller picture of all the themes first without being sidetracked by too much discussion. Second, the researchers can examine a particular finding in greater detail in the 'Discussion' section if they find it noteworthy or impactful. Perhaps, the only drawback of this approach is that in an ensuing discussion section, the researchers need to recap the specific finding later so that the reader can see the link clearly.

Referring to tables and figures

You may have noticed in research articles, researchers often include tables and figures to supplement their presentation of the results. This is especially useful when there is a huge amount of intricate information to convey. It can be rather unwieldy to present every single finding in the textual format. A table is often straightforward (i.e., with rows and columns) while a figure can be provided in the form of a bar chart, pie chart, histogram, etc. In this regard, tables and figures can help the reader maintain a helicopter view of the findings while examining each significant finding in detail. One example is as follows:

> "Four themes emerged from the days to address our research objectives: patient-perceived benefits of yoga, reasons and motivations for practising yoga, hurdles and barriers to practising yoga, and advice for effective yoga program and delivery for adult cancer. **See Table 3** for a summary of subject areas and identified patterns" (McCall et al., 2015, p. 3). (emphasis mine)

In this table, the researchers tabulated the themes and subdivided them into categories and gave instances of patterns and supporting statements. Qualitative analysis can sometimes elicit questions about being impressionistic by researchers who are not working within the same paradigm, and therefore this type of detailed tabulation serves to highlight the rigor and transparency of the analysis. This reference to the table is conveyed in a full sentence. Consider another reference to tables and figures which is shorter:

"Almost all reported acute adverse effects were associated with the musculoskeletal system (98.2%; **Fig. 1**)" (Cramer et al., 2019, p. 3). (emphasis mine)

You can see that this signposting is much more concise and unobtrusive for the reader's reading and understanding. It is to be noted that all tables and figures provided should have a corresponding reference in the main write-up. In short, figures can include bar charts, pie charts, illustrations, etc. Accompanying a table or figure is usually a corresponding label (e.g., Fig. 1), and a caption such as "Classification of acute and chronic adverse effects regarding the affected body system, the injured body parts, and the exercises associated with the injuries" (Cramer et al., 2019, p. 5).

Reporting the profile of participants, reporting findings, providing general remarks, and making reference to tables and figures are important rhetorical steps in a 'Results' section, which set up the 'Discussion' section logically.

Discussion

Statistical numbers provided are mere numbers and the thematic patterns reported are mere words without discussion or commentary. For example, if a study reports that 40% of yoga practitioners find yoga beneficial to stress management, is this considered low, moderate or high, and in relation to what? If a qualitative study found a thematic pattern that participants experience more calmness in their work, what does this mean for the specific workplace or work in general? It is thus the responsibility of researchers to provide the interpretation for readers. The Discussion section therefore answers the question of 'So what?'.

Recapitulation of key findings

At the beginning of the Discussion section, most researchers provide a recapitulation of the key findings. In Mackenzie et al.'s (2016) qualitative study of cancer survivors' and support persons' perception of a yoga program, four major themes are presented in the 'Results' section. Subsequently, in the Discussion section, the article recapitulates these main findings, as follows:

> "This set of exploratory focus groups identified the following four key thematic areas of interest in a community-based yoga for cancer survivors program, including (1) safety and shared understanding; (2) cancer-specific yoga instruction; (3) benefits of yoga participation; (4) mechanisms of yoga practice." (Mackenzie et al., 2016, p. 7)

The example above summarizes the key findings that are presented in the 'Results' section. At this juncture, you may find that this rhetorical step seems repetitive. However, in the earlier 'Results' section, these themes were supported by detailed evidence from the focus group transcripts. The recaps therefore facilitate the reader's recall of the main themes and set the stage for an organized discussion of the implications of these findings. In this regard, recaps are vital, especially in cases where the 'Results' section is separate from the 'Discussion' section in a research paper. The reader does not have to constantly turn to the previous section to review the themes. In the abovementioned example as well as in some research articles, researchers even reiterate the research objectives before summarizing key findings. This creates a smooth rhetorical flow which enables the reader to understand the article more effectively.

Making reference to past research

First, researchers may compare and/or contrast their research with past studies. These research studies are often the same sources used in the earlier literature review found in the Introduction section. If researchers are conducting a study on the perceptions of yoga teachers on rope wall yoga, they may wish to compare and contrast their findings with other research studies on rope wall yoga too. However, this does not mean that the previous studies need to have conducted a study with the exact same variables. If this current research study is the first of its kind, then the researchers may wish to compare their results with a study on a new form of yoga (e.g., aerial yoga).

In a research article, comparison with other studies can be presented in the following way. For instance, in Cheshire et al. (2022) state:

> "The improved mental and physical health reported by study participants are consistent with the significant literature citing these benefits for our patient groups [10, 13, 22, 46]. Developing self-regulation skills enabled better management of stress and improved mood, with many discussing the importance of breathing practices (pranayama) to manage emotions and stressful situations." (p. 11)

In this case, the researchers found support for their findings from four different sources, denoted by the by the numerals in square parentheses. Following the comparison provided a brief elaboration on the benefit of self-regulation skills. This is largely typical of how researchers execute this rhetorical step, which is to explain the insight briefly following a comparison to the research article. It should also be noted that researchers may employ this move many times throughout the Discussion section. It is usually easy to spot these comparison and contrast steps as they are signaled via words such as 'consistent', 'similar to', 'differ from' or 'contrasts with'. This discursive step is significant because it builds on or extends knowledge from the past, bearing in mind that research does not occur in a vacuum. It also instills more confidence in the value of a particular argument or practice.

In cases where results appear to diverge from past research, researchers may explain why this might be so. This could be due to various factors such as inherent differences in the sample, methodology, program, or research site. This is not considered a drawback of the study. Differing research findings or interpretations gives researchers a valuable opportunity chance to review the phenomenon or topic. Therefore, regardless of concordance or discordance with past studies, the discussion extends or deepens our understanding of the topic.

Discussing implications

In addition, researchers usually highlight the implications of their key findings. The figures and themes are generated by researchers' rigorous analysis. It is then up to the researchers to interpret this information meaningfully. For example, what does it mean if a study found that 60% of the participants feel that more advanced yoga classes should be conducted? Is this considered a moderate or large percentage? If the overall mean score for survey items indicating respondents' views on seated postures is 4 whereas that for standing postures is 3, does this imply participants have a stronger preference for seated postures rather than for standing postures? Is this a significant difference then? The rhetorical step of discussing implications is therefore vital because an important value of science is to make some generalizations that can be relevant and useful for mankind. Consider the following implication. Cheshire et al. (2022) state:

> "The multi-component nature of yoga **suggests** it could be an ally for improving patient activation; our qualitative data identified a number of avenues which support patient activation... Taken together these findings **suggest** that yoga may be a useful intervention for stakeholders looking to promote patient self-management and activation" (p. 11). (emphases mine)

Here, the implication is hugely positive of yoga's complementary role for helping the patient take an active role in their own health management, as well as providing a possible way for important groups of people such as yoga practitioners, yoga teachers, medical staff to incorporate this in their institutions. Implications like this one essentially answer the question of "What does this finding mean for yoga?" The insights generated are all based on solid evidence which could help them make their case to others as well. Linguistically, it is rather easy to identify implications and generalizations in the Discussion section. They are usually signposted by key reporting verbs such as 'suggest', 'imply', and 'indicate' and their associated word forms such as 'suggestion', 'implication' or 'indication'.

Application

In addition to implications, the insights derived from a study may have a more practical orientation. If a study examines participants' perception of modifications of yoga poses, a reader might expect to know which the most accessible modifications to learn are. If a study investigates participants' perceptions of instructional cues of yoga teachers, one might want to know how certain instructions may facilitate yoga students' comprehension of postures and movements so that teachers may improve their instruction in the future. Applications are therefore valuable insights with regard to how yoga teaching and learning can be better practically carried out. Here are examples to show how they may be presented in a 'Discussion' are as follows:

> "It is also recommended that individuals with specific conditions should avoid specific positions (e.g., those with hypertension or glaucoma should avoid inversion poses...)" (Cramer et al., 2019, p. 8).

> "It is important to note that in-person yoga programs do not directly translate to online platforms: they demand additional strategies for optimising safety, effectiveness and participant enjoyment" (Haynes et al., 2022, p. 9).

These insights would undoubtedly be very useful for a yoga teacher who is leading a class of students that may be more vulnerable to illnesses or faced with certain logistical constraints. A yoga practitioner who has some eye issues, for instance, may take the prudent approach of abstaining from inversion poses. In the second instance, a yoga school or center may be more mindful to evaluate how different components and aspects of the in-person program can be adapted online to maximize benefits for the students. For instance, an instructor would be more mindful to ensure the clarity of instructional cues through proper voice projection and technical management. Therefore, highlighting applications is a vital part of research.

In short, this rhetorical step answers the question: How can I apply this finding or insight realistically in yoga practice/programming/curriculum/teaching? It should be also noted that sometimes, practical applications may be included in the ensuing Conclusion section instead. They may also be known by other terms such as 'Pedagogical implications' or 'Practical applications'.

Explanation

Apart from implications, researchers may offer explanations for key or interesting findings. It is the responsibility of the researchers to explain why results turn out a certain way, especially if they are integral to the understanding of the topic or program. For example, if researchers found that a yoga intervention program did not yield the positive outcomes in the students' regulation of anxiety as well as they had hypothesized, they would probably offer some explanation. The outcome could be due to the participants' profile, content of the yoga intervention, instructors' unique styles of delivery or schedule of the yoga intervention. What is important is that researchers review their data and analysis and provide a reasonable explanation.

Here is an example of how researchers may offer an

explanation. In considering the popularity of a specially created course for seniors, Haynes et al. (2022) explained:

> "A desire to avoid unfavourable comparison to ideal body types may be one reason why classes designed exclusively for older people were welcomed by our participants. Other reasons identified in our research were that targeted classes are regarded as offering safer, achievable and more effectively tailored exercise with a community of peers". (p. 9)

Here, the study explains the popularity of the bespoke class by using their reasonable interpretation and analysis. The researchers also continue to bolster the credibility of the explanation by citing studies on customized classes and older yoga teachers. In general, researchers would also provide references to past studies that accord with their explanation. If the explanation requires more technical details, the researchers are likely to cite specific scientific studies and theories. For instance, if researchers wish to explain how they think a particular yogic exercise may have reduced stress or the propensity to obesity, they might need to link the current intervention to existing scientific research of certain body pathways to explain its efficacy. On the other hand, some explanations may not be supported with citations or theories if the matter is more logistical, such as participant attrition. This does not require a citation then. Overall, though, there is often more weight to an explanation if it can be linked to previous studies, theories, or expert opinions, as again, this extends understanding.

Limitations of the study

Many published research studies are well-planned and well-executed; however, no research is perfect. This is normal, and researchers may cover some limitations in the Discussion section. Studies can have limitations because of constraints related to access to research site, program flow, and duration allowed for the study, etc. Consider the following scenario. Researchers may wish to examine how a yoga intervention can help students improve their focus and stress management. However, the only way for them to fit it into the academic curriculum of schools may be one hour per week. Further, there may be a small number of yoga teachers that can be recruited for this program due to lack of teacher availability or financial considerations. All the abovementioned constraints could have exerted some impact on the eventual efficacy of the yoga intervention.

Most researchers tend to provide one to two limitations of the study, but they position them in a moderately positive manner:

> "While the sample in our study comprised predominantly female participants with higher educational degrees, and is thus not representative of the general population, it may be representative of yoga users given that women are more likely to practice yoga in general." (Cramer et al., 2019, p. 8)

Notice how the research still was able to highlight its value through addressing the limitation in a more positive light. The study was upfront in stating about the possible lack of representativeness to the population. However, the researchers made a good case in providing some ratio figures of male and female participation in a few countries. Rhetorically, the information on limitation is placed in the dependent clause (usually an incomplete statement) whereas the positive information is placed in the independent clause, conferring it a tenor of finality. As a result, the overall evaluation of the statement is a positive one.

Do note that limitations are not meant to negate a study. On the contrary, they invite the reader to view the study within appropriate parameters, thus managing their expectations. The researchers may make certain suggestions as to how future research can improve the response rate or sample size.

Having said that, it is also rather rare for researchers to include a series of 5 or 6 limitations in this section as this may invalidate the study instead! This has been done before but probably so in rare circumstances where a study faced significant constraints such as a very small sample size. A study is also unlikely to call these limitations 'weaknesses' as this may diminish the persuasive quality of the writing. Afterall, the entire research is meant to be a persuasive and impactful study.

Suggestions for further research

Following the limitations, future studies may be suggested to address these lacking aspects. In research studies, scientists and scholars strive to continually address weaknesses so as to improve the research design for the future. Hopefully, this will continue to break new ground, advance the respective field or discipline, and bring mankind closer and closer to the truth of the subject matter. Suggestions for future research could include refining the overall research design, including new or more diverse samples of participants, using a different instrument/equipment for measurement, etc. Scientifically again, this contributes to a future extension of the research topic and to break new ground in research. This rhetorical step enables researchers to continue the academic conversation on the topic, so to speak.

Consider the following examples to observe how suggestions for future research can be initiated. In commenting on their cancer patients' profiles, McCall et al. (2015) highlighted that only one patient out of the ten interviewees was from a cancer hospital. They pointed out:

> "The experiences or opinions of patients from other cancer care hospitals, including publicly-funded institutions may differ from this sample and should be included in further research" (p. 7).

Indeed, such suggestions remind researchers who conduct similar research in the future to take more care in their recruitment efforts to strengthen the validity of a study. Sometimes, researchers may also discover a new finding which may be beyond the scope of the current study. In that case, they may recommend another study which can examine the phenomenon in greater detail. Do also note that sometimes, the limitation section may occur outside of the 'Discussion' and appear in the 'Conclusion' instead. The following recommendation for further research occurs in a standalone section entitled 'Strengths and limitations' after the 'Discussion' section. Here, the researchers made a recommendation based on their methodology:

> "Participants were not specifically asked about individual elements of Yoga4Health classes (e.g. asana, relaxation), **future studies may wish to delve deeper** into participant

> experiences of each element, particularly the group discussion which is a unique feature of Yoga4Health." (Cheshire et al., 2022, p. 12) (emphasis mine)

We do not know why the participants were not questioned about the elements in this case. However, generally speaking, every study has specific research objectives to answer and sometimes, not every aspect of an issue, program and phenomenon can be covered. Therefore, it is best left to another research study to examine new research questions in greater depth and/or breadth. The foregoing examples demonstrate a rhetorical coupling of 'addressing limitation' and 'suggestion for future research', which is indicative of researchers' humility and continual pursuit for the truth.

Taken together, there is an understanding that scientific research is a continual endeavor that contributes to build on what preceding researchers have found. Therefore, it is an ongoing academic conversation. The Discussion section is clearly one of the most vital sections of a research article as this is where insights are provided, and knowledge becomes codified eventually.

Reading with discernment

You have learned a number of rhetorical steps in this chapter about the 'Results and Discussion'. When you are reading this section of a journal article, some questions will help you to think about the research study more critically. For example, you may ask some of the following questions: Does the report include statistics on the general profile of the participants? Are the results stated clearly? Are exact figures such as counts and percentages provided?

Are the implications reasonable or overstated? Are there any overlapping categories or information in the thematic analysis? Are the explanations logical and substantiated with supporting studies or theories? Are there any logical faults in the implications and explanations? Do the researchers discuss any limitations? Are the limitations addressed adequately? Do the limitations undermine the study in a big way?

Summary

In summary, the 'Results & Discussion' section provides the findings, tables, figures, participants' profile and offers implications, generalizations, applications, explanations, limitations and recommendations for future research. It is perhaps the most vital section of the entire paper as it paves the way for the insights to be communicated and extend the understanding of the topic. The next chapter focuses on the 'Conclusion', 'Abstract' and other miscellaneous elements.

CHAPTER 5

RESEARCH ARTICLES – CONCLUSION, ABSTRACT AND OTHER RHETORICAL ELEMENTS

The Conclusion section consolidates the entire study by highlighting the key points brought up in the earlier sections and answering the Research Questions concisely. After reading this section, the readers should have a clear understanding of whether the goal of the research has been achieved.

Imagine that a group of researchers conducts a study on the efficacy of using yoga props for yoga postures. A reader is likely to expect a statement which unequivocally answers this question. So, is the use of yoga props effective, and to what extent? Is the effectiveness applicable to most postures or only limited to certain sets of postures or only to specific postures? A reader may also wonder about the overall value of this research especially after reading the 'Results & Discussion' section. Does this study yield any useful, ambiguous or contradictory insights for knowledge and application? Since this is the last major section of the research article, it serves as the final opportunity to assert the contribution of the research study to the field or topic of study.

After reading the Conclusion, the reader may be interested in obtaining further information on the research project. They may be wondering how certain questions are being phrased in the survey and may wish to gain access to the original survey questionnaire or know which organization funds this research study. In this regard, other rhetorical elements after the Conclusion may furnish this information. On another note, a reader may wish to alert another a fellow researcher or yoga teacher who might be interested to read this research study on using props. For this purpose, a summary in the form of an Abstract may prove useful.

With the foregoing considerations in mind, we will now focus on the specific rhetorical steps in the Conclusion.

Addressing the Research Objective/Question

You would recall that in the Introduction, the objective of the research study was established. The first important rhetorical step of the Conclusion involves addressing the key research objectives or research questions. For instance, if a survey study examines elite athletes' knowledge of and attitudes toward hatha yoga, the possible research questions (RQs) may be as follows:

> RQ1: How much do elite athletes know about hatha yoga?
> RQ2: What do elite athletes think about hatha yoga?

A conclusion will answer these 2 RQs more directly. Based on the statistical analysis, researchers may state that elite athletes have very little, somewhat little, moderate amount of, somewhat sufficient or large amount of knowledge of hatha yoga, in response to RQ1. In regards to RQ2, researchers may indicate that these professional athletes have a very unfavorable, somewhat unfavorable, ambivalent, somewhat favorable or very favorable attitude toward hatha yoga. The rhetorical step of answering the research questions gives the reader a clear idea of the overall result of the research.

Here is an example of how a research objective may be addressed in a Conclusion. In response to the research aim of evaluating the acceptability and practicality of a yoga intervention, 'Yoga4Health', Cheshire et al. (2022) answer directly:

> "Yoga4Health was an **acceptable intervention** to patients …Taken together these factors suggest that **yoga is an appropriate intervention** to offer on social prescription…" (p. 12) (emphases mine)

This statement is clear in informing the readers about the suitability of the intervention. The statement was further supported with the key benefits of the intervention to the patients. Therefore, even if the readers missed out on the details in the earlier sections, they would know the crux of the research and have this as a takeaway.

Presenting key insights from Results and Discussion

Apart from having an unambiguous idea of the overall answer to the Research Objective, a research study may cover the main takeaways from the research. Referring to the preceding example on survey study, a study may mention how certain groups of athletes may tend to have more positive attitude and/or more knowledge toward hatha yoga than other groups. They may also identify the group of athletes with the most or least amount of knowledge or most or least favorable attitude toward hatha yoga. The key insights are usually not presented in greater detail than this.

Here is another example of how key insight(s) can be presented in the Conclusion section. Concluding their exploratory research on cancer patients' experience with yoga, McCall et al. (2015) pointed out:

> "As a burgeoning therapeutic intervention in adult cancer, yoga practice could **improve** aspects of patient psychological, physical and social wellbeing." (p. 8) (emphasis mine)

These three areas accord with the findings on patients' attitudes toward yoga that were reported in the Results section. They went on to summarize other findings from the study concisely. However, do take note that this is not a section where researchers discuss findings in specific detail. This has already been done in the 'Results and Discussion' section. You are also unlikely to see any statistical analysis, figures or tables in this section. The 'Conclusion' section also tends to underscore the value of the current study.

Emphasis on significance of current study

You may recall that underscoring the significance of the research study was included in the Introduction section. Taking note that this is the final main section of writing, the research article reinforces the significance of the study by emphasizing its positive qualities. In fact, as the study has made its case in the earlier sections with a rigorous methodology and sound arguments in its findings and interpretations, the tone taken by the researchers here is usually more emphatic.

Once again, with reference to the earlier hypothetical example of the survey study on knowledge of and attitudes toward hatha yoga, researchers may emphasize how this may be a first study of its kind on elite athletes as no other studies have examined this group of participants in terms of these variables systematically. They may also advocate how this study contributes to an enhanced understanding of the increasing popularity of yoga among athletes.

Notice the positive adjectives in the Conclusion sections of the following research studies:

> "The present study **generated significant contextual knowledge** about the role of yoga within cancer survivors (*sic*) lives over the course of several months within a real cancer care setting." (Mackenzie et al., 2016, p. 9) (emphases mine)

The words suggest the vital role that the current study plays in the knowledge creation process. Recall that this is important for researchers as it advances the field in terms of comprehending the significance of knowledge. The researchers continue to explain how yoga was "important" and "beneficial" to these participants (p. 9), further underlining the significance of the research. Here is another example of using words and phrases with positive associations:

> "The results of this study show **promising benefits** that are both **concrete** and **internalized** and which seem to be **culturally appropriate for diverse populations** as has

been suggested to be **important** [15, 16]."
(Wang & Hagins, 2016, p. 6) (emphases mine)

Not only did the abovementioned researchers point out the practicality of their research, they capture the potential wider impact of their research findings for yoga practitioners. In the Introduction of this study, the significance of the topic was underscored when it was highlighted that previous studies "thus far support further studies into the benefits of yoga for youth" (p. 1). Therefore, the Conclusion rounds out the research with a much more affirmative and optimistic tone. One is likely to be impressed with the idea that this research has made a huge contribution to the field.

In a research article has come full circle as the significance of a study is usually highlighted in the beginning of the article. This reiterates the value of the current study. Taken together, we can see an hour-glass rhetorical shape of the entire research article. The Introduction begins with a broad view of the topic and discussion of past research before narrowing down to the research gap which is slightly more specific and finally more specifically to the research objective and research questions. At the stem (middle portion) of this hourglass, the Methodology section contains specific details about the participants, instruments, and analytical methods. The Results section follows logically with specific analysis and details. The broadening begins slightly again at the 'Discussion' section where there is perhaps a mix of both specific information and discussion of ideas. At the broadest base of the hour-glass rhetorical shape, one may visualize the Conclusion broadening out further via by asserting the contribution of the study to the research field.

Abstract

The Abstract is a summary of the entire article. It usually consists mainly of the Introduction, Methodology, Key Findings, Discussion and Conclusion. Depending on the researchers' focus, some sections will be elaborated upon more than others.

What is the purpose of the abstract? When embarking on new research, a researcher usually sieves through hundreds of research articles to shortlist those that are relevant to him or her. Therefore, the abstract is a quick way for the researcher to ascertain its relevance without needing to read through an entire article. The vast majority of research articles contain abstracts.

Notice how the following abstract captures the entire essence of an article. I have identified the rhetorical steps in **preceding square brackets** to efficiently observe the transition from one idea to another.

[*Objective of the study*] "This study reports on the findings of a qualitative evaluation of a yoga intervention program for urban middle and high school youth in New York City public and charter schools. [*Methodology*] Six focus groups were conducted with students who participated in a year-long yoga program to determine their perceptions of mental and physical benefits as well as barriers and challenges. [*Key findings*] Results show that students perceived the benefits of yoga as increased self-regulation, mindfulness, self-esteem, physical conditioning, academic performance, and stress reduction. Barriers and challenges for a yoga practice include lack of time and space. *[Discussion]* The extent to which the benefits experienced are interrelated to one another is discussed. Suggestions for future research and school-based programming are also offered." (Wang & Hagins, 2016, p. 1)

There are a few things to note about the abstract. Firstly, it appears at the beginning of the research article. Next, it is normally assembled after the main content in the research article is completed. The abstract does not contain a literature review of past research although some abstracts do mention a research gap in the literature. Further, only key findings are mentioned, and implications of study are mentioned very briefly. Sometimes, the conclusion may be omitted, probably to avoid repetition of information already covered in the 'Results' section. This is evident from the above example. Additionally, the abstract is usually written in one continuous paragraph although some articles label the different sections.

Here are a few abstracts that include section demarcations.

- Objective- Methods-Results- Conclusions (Mackenzie et al., 2016, p. 1)
- Background-Methods-Results-Conclusion (Haynes et al., 2022, p. 1)
- Background- Methods- Results- Conclusions - Keywords (Cramer et al., 2019, p. 1).

Notice the use of different names for different sections. Typically, the first section is called objective or background. The final section can be termed in the singular or plural ('Conclusion' or 'Conclusions', respectively). In the third abstract, the authors also included a string of keywords such as "Yoga, Injuries, Adverse effects, Safety, Epidemiology" (p.

1) to enable the reader to understand the essence of the article quickly. Some journal articles publish keywords while others do not.

Other rhetorical elements

In some research, you may come across other elements that are not found in other studies. These elements usually occur after the concluding section. Here are some examples:

Conflict of interests

Imagine a scenario where a company selling yoga props and apparel conducts provides funding to research staff studying the efficacy of using yoga props in yoga classes. There is a conflict of interest here as researchers may have felt pressure, whether directly, indirectly or subconsciously in their reporting of findings. In such a research study, consumers would read it more with a skeptical eye than they would most other articles. Therefore, in many journals, researchers are required to declare any conflict of interests in their research, which can be expressed in different ways. Here are a few examples.

> "The authors declared that there is no conflict of interests." (Mason et al., 2013, p. 6)

> "The authors declare that they have no competing interests." (Cheshire et al., 2022, p. 13)

In a research study, how else might a conflict of interest arise? It may occur if the researchers accept funding from the institution that they are doing research on. Most researchers endeavor to be professional in their analysis of the research; however, it is difficult to shake off questions of potential bias in their interpretation. In the first place, most researchers would not accept the funding if they think that there is a conflict of interest or even an appearance of it. Indeed, in most studies, the funding comes from a neutral institution with interest in developing the field or research but without monetary interests.

Acknowledgements

The completion of a research study is usually the culmination of effort of a research team, advisers as well as participants. Researchers may also publicly acknowledge the help and effort others have rendered in the study, especially the participants. Some research studies may involve broaching sensitive topics (e.g., death) or special groups of people who have undergone unique treatments or experiences (e.g., rare or prolonged ailments). It is only appropriate for researchers to acknowledge these participants (as a group) then. Despite their vulnerability, these participants have generously given researchers a chance to access their world and collect data from them.

> "We warmly thank the SAGE participants who kindly took part in our process evaluation. We also thank the yoga instructors whose commitment to providing an excellent yoga program for older people, ... have made SAGE possible." (Haynes et al., 2022, p. 10).

Sometimes, the acknowledgements are an opportunity to express gratitude to the funding organization:

"The authors would like to thank the participating schools for their cooperation and support. This study was made possible through a grant awarded by the Sonima Foundation (http://www.sonimafoundation.org/)." (Wang & Hagins, 2016, p. 6)

Most research studies require funding to help them with the hiring of research associates, transcribers, the purchase of materials, booking of venues, and provision of incentives for participants. Acknowledgements like this are also important for another reason. This makes the research more transparent and credible when the readers know the source of funding and are made aware that the research is free from potential undue influence.

Appendix

You might have noticed that some research articles provide an appendix to their studies. An appendix may include a complete survey questionnaire or the complete list semi-structured interview questions. In online research articles, it is now possible to include a link to another webpage so that interested readers can view the questionnaire or other data sources that researchers have made available. Most researchers do not provide an entire survey within the main text because it is preferable for the article argument to flow more cohesively than to be displaced by a huge amount of text.

However, it is also important to note that quite a number of studies do not provide appendices for various reasons. In that case, an interested reader or researcher would have to write to the corresponding author of the study to request the survey questions.

Reading with discernment

The Conclusion and Abstracts and the miscellaneous elements are fairly straightforward sections. Some questions that may come to mind as you read them might be: Does the conclusion answer the research questions stated at the beginning of the article? Is the conclusion reasonable or overstated? Do the researchers underscore the significance of the study successfully? Does the abstract contain all the elements of the research article? Is any potential conflict of interest addressed?

Summary

The Conclusion reinforces the results of a study by addressing the research objective more directly. It is usually the last section of a long prose of writing. An abstract is a quick summary of the entire research study and covers the main structural elements: Introduction, Methods, Results & Discussion and Conclusion. How thorough the sections are covered vary across research articles. Having addressed the major components of the research article, the next chapter addresses in-text citations and the reference list, which sheds more light on the way that research is communicated.

CHAPTER 6

RESEARCH ARTICLES – CITATIONS AND REFERENCES

Citations

One of the most distinctive qualities that one can immediately notice in a research article is the use of citations that refer to other sources. As research does not occur in a vacuum, researchers often inform the reader information that has already been established surrounding the topic or theories that have been proposed regarding the topic. Citations provide the proper acknowledgment for the original sources of information. Citations are thus an important part of research writing which helps the researchers to frame their research and to continue the conversation on the topic.

There are many different academically recognized citation styles from established organizations e.g., American Mathematical Association (AMA), American Institute of Physics (AIP), American Psychological Association (APA), Chicago style etc. Some academic journals adopt one of these citation formats or dictate the use of their house style.

Therefore, researchers have to use the designated format when submitting the manuscript to an academic journal.

Regardless of the citation style, citations usually fall into 2 different format categories: numerical or author-year. Many research articles in the field of mathematics, sciences and yoga use the numerical citation format. Below is an example of numerical citation:

> "While older people are increasingly engaged with digital technologies [41] – a trend has been amplified by the COVID-19 pandemic [42] …"
>
> (Haynes et al., 2022, p. 2)

The number in the square parentheses (e.g., 42) represents a source from which the information is taken. This information about senior people is very specific and must have come from a source, be it a book, journal article, or an institutional website. This citation will have a corresponding entry in the 'Reference List' at the end of the article. If you refer to the reference page, you will notice that Reference no. 42 is a study conducted entitled "The potential for technology to enhance physical activity among older people" (p. 11). As you can see, research writing is much more precise than other forms of popular writing, and therefore more time-consuming.

It is also interesting to note that sometimes combined citations may be used, evident from the example below:

> "Teleyoga has been used with diverse populations to tackle various health conditions and has been found to be acceptable, with good adherence and positive health outcomes [28-32], …"
>
> (Haynes et al., 2022, p. 2).

This combined attribution indicates that the various sources that have been consulted generally yielded similar conclusions about these benefits of teleyoga. These suggest the relevance of these previously studies to the current one.

So far, these citations have been included immediately after a piece of information or at the end of a sentence. In some cases, the citation will appear immediately with the authors' last names. Consider the example below:

> "Similarly, Galantino et al. [17] explored the benefits of an eight-week yoga intervention for breast cancer survivors coping with aromatase inhibitor-associated arthralgias. The authors found participants experienced an increased sense of camaraderie and community within the program... Duncan [18] conducted a six-month community-based yoga intervention with a heterogenous group of cancer survivors..."
>
> (Mackenzie et al., 2016, p. 2)

In the above case, a researcher may wish to draw attention to a particular study and discuss it in some detail. This is done especially when a past research study is especially relevant to the current study. Sometimes, the decision could be based on communicative clarity. The researchers may wish to contextualize the study properly so that the reader can understand the aims clearly and see the outcomes in greater detail.

Therefore, it is dependent on the researchers' aim in that part of the writing. If the researchers' aim is to summarize the previous research findings briefly, they use the citations at the end of a phrase or sentence. If they wish to highlight a study more prominently, they will name the authors.

By and large, the research studies we have seen so far use numerical citations. However, there are research studies that use author-year citations. As you can probably tell in this book, I have been using author-year citations from the APA style to reference relevant information. The APA style is widely used in the psychological and social sciences. It is very well known and most people who have undergone some form of academic training have used it or heard of it. Although you may not use it, you might come across related articles which use an author-year style. Therefore, it is still essential to understand this style.

For the purpose of illustration, I can reference a piece of information as follows:

> Exercise is essential to physical and mental well-being (Brown, 2022).
>
> Brown (2022) asserts that exercise is essential to physical and mental well-being.
>
> Exercise has shown many benefits (Brown, 2023; Lee, 2022).

As you can tell, these citations are very similar to the numerical system. In a combined citation, the two works will be separated by a punctuation mark which may be comma or a semi-colon, depending on the citing convention.

Now that the in-text citation is covered, we will proceed to the 'References' section.

References

A reference list contains references that correspond to the citations in the main article. The References section is typically arranged in ascending numbers for the numerical citation format. This section is often found at the end of the article or at the end of a book.

We will look at three references to understand the anatomy of a reference entry. The first reference entry is for a journal article.

> [19] M. McCall, S. Thorne, A. Ward, and C. Heneghan, "Yoga in adult cancer: an exploratory qualitative analysis of the patient experience," *BMC Complementary and Alternative Medicine*, vol. 15, no. 1, article 245, 2015.
>
> (Mackenzie et al., 2016, p. 10)

In this reference, the authors are listed according to their first name initial and family name. The four researchers' names are separated by commas. This is followed by the title of the research article, and subsequently, the journal title. You would notice that the first letter of essential words is usually capitalized. The volume number '15' in which this journal article is found is then listed, followed by the issue number which is 1 in this case. In this particular journal, the articles are designated numbers. Lastly, the year of publication is provided. Some references also indicate the page numbers while others do not.

It is essential to understand the above convention because the journal article is the most common source being cited in most research articles. The next reference entry which requires understanding is an academic book:

> [24] J. W. Cresswell, *Qualitative Inquiry and Research Design: Choosing among Five Approaches,* Sage, 2012.
>
> (Mackenzie et al., 2016, p. 10)

This citation consists of the author, whose first name initials and family name are provided. This is followed by the book title, publishing company, and the year of publication.

As we have mentioned at the beginning of this book, researchers may also consult institutional websites. Here is an example of an entry in the reference list:

> 6. Cancer Research UK, United Kingdom: Yoga. Available at http://www.cancerresearchuk. org/cancer-help/about-cancer/treatment/ complementary-alternative/therapies/yoga
>
> (McCall et al., 2015, p. 9)

The components of this reference entry are rather straightforward. It lists the institutional author (Cancer Research UK, United Kingdom) followed by the information title of the webpage (Yoga), and lastly the url.

As far as possible, researchers will try to list all the required components in a reference entry. This is to enable other readers and researchers to locate the source easily for further reading. However, do take note that the web addresses to some links may change over time, which makes the exact location more difficult.

Reading with discernment

Again, as you are reading a journal article of your choice, certain citations and references to other studies might catch your attention. You might want to read up on another study. Certain questions that can guide you are as follows. Are all the sources of information used mostly academic sources? Are the sentences in the article that mention specific information accompanied by citations? Does every citation have a corresponding entry in the reference list? Does the research article use mainly journal articles? Are many of the works cited authored by the researchers themselves? And if so, will that cause any bias? Are sufficient citations from other works included?

Summary

Citations and references are essential in a research article as they give the original sources of information due acknowledgment. The way that in-text citations are integrated with the sentences have their specific rhetorical functions. Each citation has a corresponding entry in the reference list that enables researchers to look them up if more information is required. In sum, citations and references constitute an integral part of the culture and language of a research community. The next chapter examines specifically the language of research writing in research articles.

CHAPTER 7

THE LANGUAGE OF
RESEARCH ARTICLES

The previous chapters have focused on the rhetorical steps of the research articles. In this chapter, we turn our attention to the language features of research articles. More often than not, I have heard novice researchers comment with a tone of protest: "Why do researchers write in this way? It's so difficult to read."

One has to appreciate that research writing is more precise, and therefore words are chosen more carefully than in a piece of popular writing. The tenor of formality is definitely more pronounced than that of a blog entry, magazine article or an SMS text. In this chapter, a few language features are covered to enable the reader to appreciate the style of research writing and become more adept at navigating the research article.

Passive Voice

One of the common language features of research writing is the use of the passive voice. Here, the difference between the active and passive voice is shown:

> "A total of 4 yoga teachers' associations, 3 congress organizers, and 145 yoga studios were contacted and asked to send the link of the survey to their members or customers."
> (Cramer et al., 2019, p. 2)

The passive voice typically fronts the object elements to highlight their prominence. The important elements are the associations, congress organizers and studios, not the researchers or administrators.

In contrast, a sentence in an active voice would start the sentence: "The researchers contacted and asked a total of 4 yoga teachers' associations, ... to send the link..." The spotlight in the sentence would have shifted to the researchers instead.

Some might say there is really very little difference here. However, the passive voice is used for good reason. The preceding sentence was about the participants in the study and specifically mentioned these three sites from which participants were recruited. Therefore, the passive voice in the subsequent sentence maintains this coherence of ideas and cohesiveness of writing, instead of throwing off the focus.

Do note that the passive voice can also accomplish something that the active voice could not. Consider these sentences:

- Example 1: The researchers entered the data into the SPSS program.

- Example 2: The results were entered into the SPSS program by the researchers.
- Example 3: The results were entered into the SPSS program.

Example 1 shows that the initiators of the action need to be included in an active voice because it is not grammatical to start with "entered the data...". Examples 2 and 3 illustrate the passive voice. Example 2 includes the initiators at the end of the sentence, but it is not crucial. In contrast, Example 3 does not include the initiators and allows the reader to focus squarely on the results.

The overall effect, then, is that the researchers are able to come across as more objective and dispassionate in their research writing through the omission of the initiators. This is congruent with the scientific endeavor where objectivity is valued.

However, the culture of academic and research writing can shift over time. More and more researchers are favoring the use of the active voice as a more straightforward way of expression. Whatever the language choice might be, it is important that the researcher understands the impact of their language use.

Nominalization

Next, we turn our attention to nominalization. This is commonly done in research writing and for good reason. Nominalization is the transformation of verbs or adjectives to nouns. Put simply, verbs such as "create" will be changed to "creation". Adjectives such as "effective" will be converted to "effectiveness".

Observe how this sentence consists of nouns and noun phrases instead of verbs.

> "Scheduling, transportation, lack of time and competing priorities were listed as key barriers to attending regular yoga class." (McCall et al., 2015, p. 6)

The nominalizations are "scheduling", "transportation", "lack of time", "competing priorities", "key barriers" and "attending regular yoga class". You might have noticed that the whole tenor of the sentence sounded formal and even authoritative. This is because nominalizations have essentially turned these verbs into concepts. Scientists and researchers frequently communicate in terms of ideas, concepts and theories. This enables them to discuss these ideas easily throughout a text.

So, instead of having three separate sentences, you now have a concise sentence packed with ideas. It is definitely not wrong to communicate in this way:

> The participants conveyed that they could not schedule yoga into their busy lives, and they often lacked the time for yoga. Furthermore, they could not commute efficiently to the studios and their various priorities often compete with one another. As a result, they could not attend yoga class regularly.

However, the concepts and ideas are not readily apparent here, and the reader needs to gather the ideas on their own. Nominalization helps to summarize and synthesize the ideas effectively.

Having said this, it is also important to note that an overuse of nominalization can be problematic. In an academic text, the discussion of ideas is paramount. However, in a text that requires more storytelling or description, verbs and adjectives are preferable. This is why in the early years of education, nominalization do not feature prominently in extended texts. If they do occur, they often create reading and comprehension difficulties for the student. At this level of research writing, however, nominalization is appropriate for the discussion of ideas and concepts.

Qualifying language

Qualifying language refers to words and phrases that adjust the intensity and certainty of what one wishes to communicate. This means that researchers may use certain words such as "may", "possible" or "likely" to convey the certainty of their claims and conclusions.

Some might ask: Isn't research based on facts? Isn't research supposed to be sure about whether certain beverages are beneficial or detrimental to health? On that note, I would encourage you to read the conclusions in many scientific articles again, be they in the popular arena or in academic research. Medical researchers would probably not state, for instance, caffeine intake *cures* headaches. Instead, the research article is more likely to state, "Drinking **certain teas can alleviate** headaches". In this regard, the researcher is using qualifying language to be as accurate as possible and responsible to the public who may consume this information. Consider some of the following examples where the qualifiers are emboldened for easy reference.

"Better understanding of how older people perceive and engage with teleyoga... **can** inform strategies for improved design, implementation and promotion of teleyoga and other online exercise programs [48, 49]." (Haynes et al., 2022, p. 2)

In the introductory section above, the researchers do not use "will" or "must", but use "can" to signpost a possibility and capacity of how understanding seniors can contribute to better program design, thus opening up the space for some discussion. Apart from "can", modal verbs like "may", "could", and "should" are often employed by researchers to hedge their statements. Here is an example of how "may" is used when discussing limitations of a study:

"First the issue of true confidentiality as well as social desirability **may** have impacted the students' ability to be completely honest and open. Although the yoga teachers and school personnel were not present for any part of the focus groups, …. there **may** still have been resistance to speak freely." (Wang & Hagins, 2016, p. 5)

In this case, this modal verb enables the researchers to offer factors that could have affected the study so that the reader gets a complete picture of the research. Apart from "can" and "may", "should" is often used by researchers:

"Quantitative studies including clinical trials, **should** now be used to explore this intervention further, our findings can be used to guide the design of such research." (Cheshire et al., 2022, p. 12)

As can be seen from the above statement, this modal verb is stronger in tone and is often associated with advice-giving, suggestions for improvement and recommendations. Other modal verbs include "might", "could", "would", "ought to", which are more tentative. In the above sentence, the researchers did not use "must" or "will" as these are absolute.

Other types of qualifying language include the use of verbs such as "seem", "appear", "suggest", "imply" and "assume". Observe how these verbs are appropriately employed when offering certain generalizations and implications:

> "Indeed, the group element of the Yoga4Health programme **appeared** to act as vehicle for informational, emotional and social support" (Cheshire et al., 2022, p. 11).

The qualifying language highlights the impact of the group component of the programme with confidence and humility simultaneously. In fact, the choice of the verb "act", instead of stronger verbs like "serve" or "function", further signals some room for negotiation in regards to its impact. Consider another example which is used in the Conclusion section:

> "These results **suggest** that some form of regular or formal supervisory guidance may be beneficial for reducing adverse events associated with yoga practice." (Cramer et al., 2019, p. 8)

Notice how suggest was being used instead of a more definite verb such as "show". It seems likely that the researchers are cautious and responsible here. The researchers have found that there is a stronger likelihood of injury when practicing yoga without supervision. The use of this qualifier in the above implication thus leaves some room for debate and negotiation. A reader may think of exceptions, such as in the case where practitioners do not like monitoring from others when doing yoga. This might be counter-productive for the practitioner, then.

After reading this section, you will be much attuned to discovering more and more modal verbs throughout research articles. Therefore, these verbs enable the researchers to communicate with some measure of confidence and uncertainty.

We will look at one final set of expressions associated with qualifying language. This group consists of adjectives, adverbs and nominalizations. They include "possible", "potential" and "likely". Researchers attempt to be cautious, especially when offering explanations. Here is an example of how improved baroreflex sensitivity (BRS) might have come about in a study on yogic slow breathing by Mason et al. (2013)

"In this study, we show that slow breathing and increased oxygen absorption lead to enhanced BRS. This might result from several **possible** factors, all interrelated." (p. 5)

The researchers went on to offer a theory which was supported by an observation in another past study. Indeed, these expressions are ideal when surmising with confidence or offering advice.

Consider the use of the word 'potential' in the following:

"As such the use of props cannot be considered hazardous in general, however precautions should be applied when practicing with props, such as ensuring correct handling of props (including securing the props when they are not used), and not applying props to push and exceed bodily limitations, to reduce **potential** yoga-associated adverse events." (Cramer et al. 2019, p. 8.)

Imagine if the word "potential" is omitted. The advisory might have come across as too absolute. Not everyone will experience adverse effects in yoga practice. By including the qualifier, the researcher is also able to alert the yoga practitioner more effectively that various scenarios can occur, and the examples listed are not exhaustive. A qualifier may only be a word, but it makes a huge difference in the argument.

We'll turn our focus to another qualifier "likely". This term is particularly useful when underscoring the significance of a study or program:

> "Specific activities to support the social cohesion of a yoga group (e.g., time for discussion), as delivered by Yoga4Health, are **likely** to maximise these social benefits, the importance of which may be currently under-estimated." (Cheshire et al., 2022, p. 11)

Of course, the term "likely" can be used in the context of discussing implications or offering explanations:

> "Enjoyment is **likely** to be key to sustaining engagement and benefits of an intervention by increasing intrinsic motivation [60, 61]." (Cheshire et al., 2022, p 11)

Noteworthy here is that the term "likely" is used often by these researchers in the discussion section. The use of this term provides a more forward-looking and confident tenor than many other hedges such as "seem" or "may".

In my opinion, "likely" can be used more often by

researchers, especially toward the end of a Discussion section and the Conclusion section. Since researchers have normally made their case up till this point, sufficient evidence should have been accrued. Using "likely" then underscores the researchers' confidence in the study.

Undoubtedly, there are many ways of expressing these qualifiers:

- possible (adjective), possibly (adverb), possibility (noun)
- potential (adjective), potentially (adverb)
- likely (adjective or adverb), likelihood (noun)

For instance, I can state the same thing in different ways:

Diaphragmatic breathing is **likely** [adjective] to help calm a person's nerves before an important performance.

Diaphragmatic breathing most **likely** [adverb] helps calm a person's nerves before an important performance.

There is a strong **likelihood [noun]** that diaphragmatic breathing helps calm a person's nerves before an important performance.

The choice of words may be dependent on the preceding sentences, ensuing sentences, rhetorical purpose, and overall authorial style of the research article.

Formal Vocabulary

Perhaps one of the most prominent features of research writing is the use of technical jargon and formal words. This feature enables researchers to convey their ideas with precision. In their abstract, Mason et al., (2013) described the Ujjayi breath:

> "Within the yoga tradition slow breathing is often paired with a contraction of the glottis muscles. This resistance breath "ujjayi" is performed at various rates and ratios of inspiration/expiration." (Mason et al., 2013, p. 1)

Notice the use of the official name for the breath "ujjayi", as opposed to "ocean breath" or "victorious breath" used in common parlance. Here, the main features of the breath are concisely described. Subsequently, the terms "inspiration/expiration" are used instead of "inhalation/exhalation" or even more conversational ones such as "breathing in" and "breathing out".

Apart from using more technical terms, research writing often employs the use of more formal vocabulary. Consider the following example:

> "Social prescribing is a means of enabling general practitioners and other primary healthcare professionals to formally refer patients to a range of non-clinical community services." (Cheshire et al., 2022, pp. 1-2).

In less formal texts and speech, the word "means" can be replaced with "ways", enabling can be replaced with "helping", "general practitioners" with "G.P.s" and "a range of" with "many different". However, the academic vocabulary lends gravitas and accuracy in the researchers' definition of the term "social prescribing". It is not that plain English does not communicate these effectively.

You may also notice that this sentence is expressed in a long, nominalized phrase beginning with " a means of..." and ending with "services". Therefore, apart from the vocabulary, the grammatical and sentence structure is also slightly longer than most non-research genres. This is because in research articles, researchers aim to be insightful and comprehensive; therefore, they tend to identify links between ideas and components. In this regard, the formal vocabulary and sentence sophistication go in hand in hand.

Reading with discernment

As you are reading the research article, some questions like these may come to mind. Do the research articles that you have read use qualifying language appropriately? Is there anywhere in the research's article that you feel that the researchers could have used better qualifiers? Are the nominalizations used appropriately? Is there anywhere in the text where the excessive use of nouns and noun phrases affect the readability of the text? Does the research article use formal vocabulary where necessary? Are there overly short sentences which are not linked properly to show the connection of ideas? Are there overly long sentences that impede understanding of the concepts?

Summary

In this chapter, language features such as passive voice, nominalization, qualifying language and formal vocabulary are covered. These features are not frivolous but carefully used to convey ideas with accuracy, precision, guarded confidence and gravitas. In well-established groups such as research communities, the language usage is congruent with the ideals and principles of the scientific community and endeavor.

CHAPTER 8

CONSOLIDATION

By now, you would have realized that a research article is not merely a document filled with information but one that is written with rhetorical purposes to inform the reader meaningfully and persuasively.

The Introduction sets the stage for the research and provides background information about the topic and some current information about the site of research. The literature review is usually subsumed within the Introduction although occasionally it is a section on its own. More importantly, this section enables the researcher to identify a gap in research and highlight how the current study fills the gap through its research objective and research questions. The Methodology section covers information on the participants, materials, instruments, data collection process, and the method of analysis. This segues logically into the 'Results and Discussion' section where analyses are presented along with tables and figures, and their implications, explanations, impact, and limitations are discussed. The Conclusion section provides the answer to the research questions directly. The significance of the study is once again emphasized and its contribution to the study reinforced.

With this understanding, it is also helpful to reiterate the alternative names of some sections and subsections.

- Introduction - This section sometimes contains a subsection named 'Background'.
- Methodology - This may be known as 'Methods'. It may also contain subsections such as 'Data collection' or 'Methods of Analysis', depending on the nature of the project.
- Results & Discussion - This section may be separated into two different ones. The 'Results' section may be known as 'Findings', and the 'Discussion' section stands on its own.
- Conclusion - This may be known as General Discussion.
- Abstract – This name is rather standard across academic journals.

Depending on the editorial direction of the academic journal, the journal may use different names for the respective sections and have slight variations in the content types. It is also true that some research articles may not contain some of the rhetorical steps that are covered above. For instance, although it is traditionally important to include a research gap, some articles do not include it. Nevertheless, it is vital for us to understand the overall structure and the possible rhetorical steps in research articles.

Apart from knowing the rhetorical purposes of the various sections, you have also gained access to the conventions of research writing. By and large, the use of certain citations and references is dependent on the editorial direction of the chosen academic journal. On a more micro-level, the decision of certain placement of in-text citations within sentences rests upon the authors' rhetorical purposes, for example, summarizing a group of studies or accentuating a certain study. Correspondingly, the reference list enables readers to locate the source of information should they wish to know more about the subject matter.

In this book, you have also learned the metalanguage of research writing. The use of passive voice enables the researcher to communicate their research in a more objective, dispassionate manner through fronting the relevant subject matter. Nominalization, the use of nouns and noun phrases, allows the researchers to port the concept or idea around the article and interact with other ideas for efficient discussion. Qualifying language enables researchers to make extrapolations and discuss implications with guarded confidence. Indeed, the findings on yoga in the study may be supported, disputed, or refuted by future studies. The use of qualifiers provides room for discussion and negotiation on these results and interpretations. More broadly speaking, this act of humility brings about transparency and open-mindedness in intellectual discourse, and hopefully brings all researchers and readers closer to the truth of the matter. The use of technical jargon and formal vocabulary lends precision in definition, explanation and discussion of the subject matter, as well as provides a tenor of dignity and gravitas to the entire research endeavor.

Indeed, the insights derived from research studies help inform the practice and teaching of yoga. This lends confidence and assuredness on the one hand and allows us to continually evaluate and reassess certain ways of doing yoga. Reading various research articles on yoga opens our hearts and minds into how yoga can make a difference in diverse populations and groups of people situated in various physical, mental, psychological, and emotional circumstances. Since no one can truly know fully about a subject, keeping up with recent research enables us to inform ourselves more richly about the vast potentialities and possibilities of yoga.

REVIEW QUIZ

1. Which of the following is least likely to be considered a part of research study in yoga?

   a. Administering a survey questionnaire to participants
   b. Discussing the impact of a yoga program on participants
   c. Reviewing scholarly literature on a yoga practice
   d. Writing a blog post about a yoga retreat

2. Who/What determines the method that yoga researchers would use to collect the data for their research?

   a. The academic journal
   b. The study research objective/questions
   c. The yoga center
   d. The participants

3. Yoga researchers communicate their research findings through

   a. an academic journal
   b. a newspaper

c. a conversation

d. a magazine

4. Which of the following factors do yoga researchers consider when deciding on a research topic?

   a. originality
   b. impact
   c. access to research site
   d. all of the above

5. What are the main deciding factors for a reputable journal to publish a research article?

   a. editors' decision and peer review
   b. length and breadth of article
   c. duration of study and conflict of interest
   d. researcher' track record and acknowledgments

6. Which of the following is an academic source?

   a. A store website selling yoga attire
   b. A magazine article on the benefits of yoga
   c. A handbook on yoga practices
   d. A blog on yogic breathing

7. Academic researchers may cite a particular newspaper article

   a. to make reference to an event that happened
   b. to make reference to a particular research study
   c. to make reference to past literature
   d. none of the above

8. What is likely to happen when a research manuscript gets rejected by the research journal for publication?

   a. The researchers submit the manuscript again to the same academic journal for consideration after making amendments.
   b. The researchers conduct the research study again and then rewrite the research article.
   c. The researchers may make amendments to the manuscript and submit to another academic journal.
   d. All of the above are possible solutions.

9. In the 'Introduction' section of a research article,

   a. researchers describe the sampling method.
   b. researchers recommend areas for improvement.
   c. researchers provide some background information.
   d. researchers discuss the limitations of the study.

10. Why do researchers identify a research gap?

   a. To extend what is missing in past literature through the current study
   b. To link it to the relevance of the results of the current study
   c. To consider the method of analysis for the current study
   d. To provide a helicopter view of the current study

11. Which of the following is a research objective?

   a. The aim of this study is to examine the opinions of yoga teachers toward acro yoga.
   b. Research has shown that practicing restorative yoga has health benefits.

c. This research on yoga nidra will describe the recruitment process and instruments followed by the method of analysis.
d. Please refer to the table for a complete profile of the yoga practitioners who participate in this survey on acro yoga.

12. Readers may critically evaluate the 'Introduction' using one of the following questions:

a. Is the conclusion of the study sound?
b. Do the researchers make a successful case for the significance of the study?
c. Is the interpretation of the results of the current study sound?
d. None of the above

13. Why do researchers usually interview only a sample of the population, but not the entire population?

a. There is a fixed number of participants for a research study.
b. The methodology is qualitative, not quantitative.
c. This is determined by the sampling method.
d. In some cases, it is impossible to interview everyone.

14. Why is random sampling not preferred in some research?

a. It is too random and convenient.
b. It is not considered a scientific or rigorous method.
c. It is very difficult to perform random sampling using existing statistical software.
d. The final sample may over-represent one particular section of the sample, which can lead to bias.

15. Which of the following can be considered an instrument/ instruments?

   a. Survey Questionnaire
   b. Focus Group Interview Script
   c. Written Test
   d. All of the above

16. Which of the following does not belong to a 'Results & Discussion' section?

   a. Discussing data collection
   b. Referring to tables or figures
   c. Presenting main findings
   d. Making a general remark

17. In a standalone 'Discussion' section, why is it important for researchers to recap the results?

   a. To highlight how important it is
   b. To discuss them in a systematic manner
   c. To make a conclusion about them
   d. To discuss the limitations

18. When discussing the limitations, researchers usually

   a. list many limitations to be comprehensive
   b. label them as weaknesses
   c. address them in a positive light
   d. gloss over details as it may decrease credibility of the study

19. Some findings may generate new insights that go beyond the scope of study. What might researchers do?

    a. Researchers might recommend them for future research.
    b. Researchers might discuss the findings with limitations.
    c. Researchers might conduct a review of the literature.
    d. Researchers might shift them to the abstract.

20. When offering an explanation for a finding,

    a. researchers may cite a study to support their explanation.
    b. researchers may cite a theory to substantiate their explanation.
    c. researchers may offer a reasonable argument without citation.
    d. all of the above

21. Why do researchers compare and contrast their findings with other studies?

    a. To extend understanding of the topic
    b. To generate the conclusion to their own study
    c. To summarize their findings
    d. To prevent any conflict of interest

22. Which of the following is least likely to be a limitation of a study?

    a. The sample size of the participants is too small.
    b. The researchers only managed to get the permission of one institute to conduct their study on the participants.

c. The sample size contained participants who were of a certain social economic status (SES)

d. The study was not based on any theories or literature.

23. Which of the following is not a rhetorical step in the 'Results and Discussion' section?

a. Researchers may refer to a table.
b. Researchers may describe the method.
c. Researchers may refer to a chart.
d. Researchers may present the main findings.

24. Which of the following is usually a rhetorical step in the Conclusion?

a. Reviewing past literature
b. Identifying a research gap
c. Critiquing the data collection
d. Reiterating the significance of the study

25. Why is it important to declare any conflict of interests?

a. To declare that the results are free from potential external interference
b. To convince readers that the study is original
c. To make sure that the research participation is voluntary
d. All of the above

26. Which of the following is not true about an abstract?

a. It is a summary of the research study.
b. It is written first before other sections by the researchers.

c. It helps other researchers decide if the research article is relevant to their research study
d. All of the above

27. Which of the following is a nominalization in this sentence?

Sentence: There is a reasonable assumption that yoga practitioners tend to respect one another's space in a yoga class.

a. tend
b. reasonable
c. assumption
d. respect

28. Which of the following words is/are a qualifier(s) in the sentence?

Sentence: Therefore, the practice of yoga nidra is likely to be a major contributing factor for the participants' daily experience of calmness.

a. likely
b. Therefore
c. calmness
d. all of the above

29. Which of the following sentences contains the use of passive voice?

a. Consider these factors that affect the recruitment of participants for the yoga study.
b. The study was conducted over ten years and follow-up interviews were conducted with the yoga participants.

c. The researchers assign the yoga participants into three groups: one which underwent the yoga program, another which listened to the guided meditation, and a third group which only had their usual academic classes without any complementary modality.

d. The organisers have offered a variety of reasons for the lack of participation in this new style of yoga.

30. What is the biggest flaw in the following sentence?

Sentence: Overall, perhaps, there may be a range of factors which could have probably affected the ostensibly the attrition rate of this yoga class.

a. There is an overuse of the passive voice.
b. There is an overuse of nominalization.
c. There is an overuse of qualifiers.
d. There is an overuse of academic vocabulary.

31. In a study, the participants are usually promised

a. confidentiality
b. anonymity
c. results
d. flexibility of schedule

32. If researchers have a list of participants and categorize them according to their socioeconomic status in order to sample the participants, this is an example of

a. random sampling
b. snowball sampling
c. systematic sampling
d. stratified sampling

33. Why is it important to provide definitions?

    a. Researchers need to use it to describe the method of data collection.
    b. Researchers can have a point of reference to discuss the subject matter meaningfully.
    c. Researchers need it to derive the method of analysis.
    d. Researchers can use it to provide an overview of the research.

34. There are normally two types of citation styles for academic journal articles: numerical and _____.

    a. author-date
    b. author-number
    c. author-year
    d. author-publishing house

35. For every citation that appears in the main text of a research article, there is an entry in the _____ at the end of the article.

    a. reference list
    b. glossary
    c. appendix
    d. table

ANSWERS TO REVIEW QUIZ

1. d
2. b
3. a
4. d
5. a
6. c
7. a
8. c
9. c
10. a
11. a
12. h
13. d
14. d
15. d
16. a

17. b

18. c

19. a

20. d

21. a

22. d

23. b

24. d

25. a

26. b

27. c

28. a

29. b

30. c

31. a

32. d

33. b

34. c

35. a

CONTINUING EDUCATION

Congratulations! You have reached the last chapter of the book.

You are now equipped with a much better understanding of the research process and the research article on yoga. This is a valuable skill which will help you to select and evaluate information more judiciously as you navigate research.

What a time for us to be living in, when access to both research and yoga is flourishing. Indeed, we are fortunate and privileged to be learning, growing, and living in and through these invaluable disciplines and resources.

If you feel inspired to learn more, please visit Yoga Well at the url: www.yogawell.co for more information.

On this website, you can find various courses or coaching sessions on yoga, nlp, and applied linguistics. If you have any questions or comments, simply reach out to me via the following:

Website email: info@nlpyogawell.com
Website: https://nlpyogawell.com
Instructor's email: drethansee@gmail.com

Once again, I wish you the very best in your future endeavors.

BIBLIOGRAPHY

This is a list of research articles that are cited in this book.

Cheshire, A., Richards, R., & Cartwright, T. (2022). 'Joining a group was inspiring': A qualitative study of service users' experiences of yoga on social prescription. *BMC Complementary Medicine and Therapies, 22*: 67. https://doi.org/10.1186/s12906-022-03514-3

Cramer, H., Quinker, D., Schumann, D., Wardle, J., Dobos, G., & Lauche, R. (2019). Adverse effects of yoga: a national cross-sectional survey. *BMC Complementary and Alternative Medicine, 19*: 190. https://doi.org/10.1186/s12906-019-2612-7

Haynes, A., Gilchrist, H., Oliveira, J. S., Sherrington, C., & Tiedemann, A. (2022). "I wouldn't have joined if it wasn't online". Understanding older people's engagement with teleyoga classes for fall prevention. *BMC Complementary Medicine and Therapies, 22*: 283. https://doi.org/10.1186/s12906-022-03756-1

Mackenzie, M. J., Wurz, A. J., Yamauchi, Y., Pires, L. A., & Culos-Reed, S. N. (2016). Yoga helps put the pieces back together: A qualitative exploration of a community-based yoga program for cancer survivors. *Evidence-Based Complementary and Alternative Medicine*. Volume 2016, Article ID 1832515. https://dx.doi.org/10.1155/2016/1832515

Mason, H., Vandoni, M., deBarbieri, G., Codrons, E., Ugargol, V., & Bernardi, L. (2013). Cardiovascular and respiratory effect of yogic slow breathing in the yoga beginner: What is the best approach? *Evidence-Based Complementary and Alternative Medicine*. Volume 2013, Article ID 743504. https://dx.doi.org/10.1155/2013/743504

McCall, M., Thorne, S., Ward, A., & Heneghan, C. (2015). Yoga in adult cancer: An exploratory, qualitative analysis of the patient experience. *BMC Complementary and Alternative Medicine*, *15*: 245. https://doi.org/10.1186/s12906-015-0738-9

Wang, D., & Hagins, M. (2016). Perceived benefits of yoga among urban school students: A qualitative analysis. *Evidence-Based Complementary and Alternative Medicine*. Volume 2016, Article ID 8725654. https://dx.doi.org/10.1155/2016/8725654

The definition of 'research' is derived from the following source.

Research. (2023). In *Merriam-Webster's online dictionary*. Retrieved from https://www.merriam-webster.com/dictionary/research

ABOUT THE AUTHOR

Ethan See, PhD is an educator of Applied Linguistics, Neurolinguistic Programming (NLP) and Yoga. He has a wealth of experience in teaching academic communication and scientific writing to undergraduates and graduate students. He has authored articles and books related to linguistics and scientific communication and has served as reviewer for academic journals. Overall, he has vast experience in the field of English Language Teaching (ELT), having taught students from absolute beginners to doctoral degree students.

Dr See is passionate about Yoga, personal development and self-care. He is a personal development coach who uses Yoga and NLP modalities to help others achieve more abundance and wellness in their life. At the heart of Dr See's teaching is the significant role of words and discourse in everyday life, which explains the transformative impact that powerful modalities such as NLP, Yoga Nidra and meditation have on people's lives.

For more information on courses and coaching sessions offered by Dr Ethan See and teaching associates, please reach out via the following:

Website email: info@nlpyogawell.com
Website: https://nlpyogawell.com
Instructor's email: drethansee@gmail.com